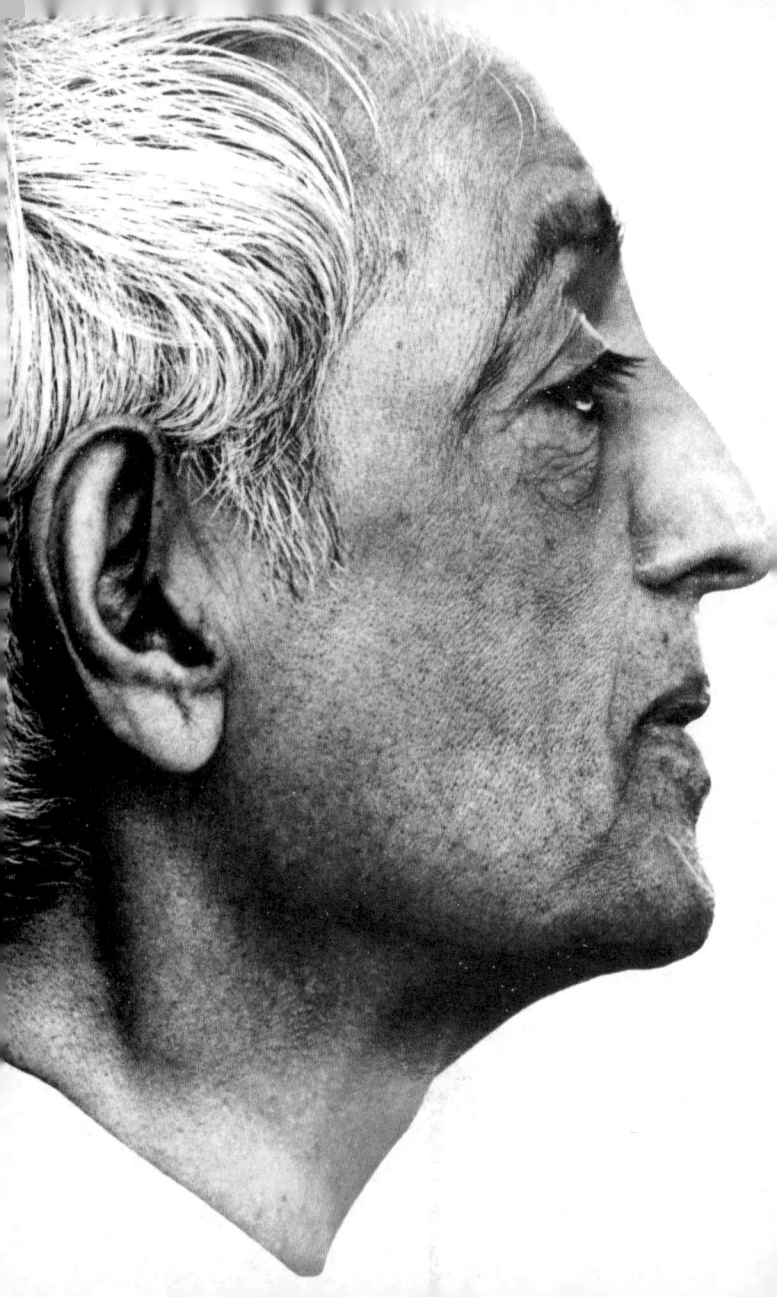

Education
and the
Significance
of Life

唤醒智慧的教育

[印] 吉杜·克里希那穆提 著　周豪 译

重庆出版社

Education and the Significance of Life
Copyright © 1953 Krishnamurti Foundation of America
Krishnamurti Foundation of America
P.O.Box 1560, Ojai, California 93024 USA
E-mail: kfa@kfa.org. Website: www.kfa.org
Simplified Chinese edition copyright © BEIJING ALPHA BOOKS CO., INC., 2024
All rights reserved including the rights of reproduction in whole or in part in any form.

版贸核渝字（2024）第155号

图书在版编目（CIP）数据

唤醒智慧的教育 /（印）吉杜·克里希那穆提著；周豪译. -- 重庆：重庆出版社，2025.3. -- ISBN 978-7-229-19011-8

Ⅰ．G4-53

中国国家版本馆CIP数据核字第2024NY2049号

唤醒智慧的教育
HUANXING ZHIHUI DE JIAOYU
[印] 吉杜·克里希那穆提 著　周豪 译

出　　品：	华章同人
出版监制：	徐宪江　连　果
责任编辑：	彭圆琦
责任校对：	王昌凤
营销编辑：	史青苗　冯思佳
责任印制：	梁善池
书籍设计：	潘振宇 774038217@qq.com

重庆出版集团
重庆出版社　出版

（重庆市南岸区南滨路162号1幢）
北京博海升彩色印刷有限公司　印刷
重庆出版集团图书发行公司　发行
邮购电话：010-85869375
全国新华书店经销
开本：710mm×1000mm　1/32　印张：9.75　字数：126千
2025年3月第1版　2025年3月第1次印刷
定价：49.80元

如有印装问题，请致电023-68706683
版权所有　侵权必究

无知之人并不是没有学问的人，
而是不了解自己的人。

**The ignorant man is not the unlearned,
but he who does not know himself.**

目录

第一章

教育与生活的意义 /010

教育不仅仅是获取知识,收集各种事实数据然后把它们关联起来;
教育是看到生活作为一个整体的意义所在。

第二章

正确的教育 /028

正确的教育在于如实地了解孩子,而不是把我们认为"他应该怎样"的理想强加在他身上。

第三章

智力、权威和智慧 /118

我们自己的想法才是最重要的,而不是别人想要我们去想的东西。

第四章

教育与世界和平 /164

如果我们希望建立一个真正开明的社会,
就必须要有一些了解达到完整的途径的教育者,
由此他们就能够把那份了解传递给孩子。

CONTENTS

CHAPTER I

EDUCATION AND THE SIGNIFICANCE OF LIFE /010

Education is not merely acquiring knowledge, gathering correlating facts; it is to see the significance of life as a whole.

CHAPTER II

THE RIGHT KIND OF EDUCATION /028

The right kind of education consists in understanding the child as he is without imposing upon him an ideal of what we think he should be.

CHAPTER III

INTELLECT, AUTHORITY AND INTELLIGENCE /118

It is what we think that matters, not what others want us to think.

CHAPTER IV

EDUCATION AND WORLD PEACE /164

If we wish to build a truly enlightened society, we must have educators who understand the ways of integration and who are therefore capable of imparting that understanding to the child.

第五章

学校 /196

我们大部分人都想要大型的学校,里面尽是一幢幢威风的大楼——即使它们显然并不是正确的教育中心。

第六章

父母和老师 /236

因此,问题不在孩子,而在父母和老师;
问题在于要去教育那个教育者。

第七章

性与婚姻 /280

性是属于头脑的,而属于头脑的事物必定要让自己得到满足,否则它就会感到挫败。

第八章

艺术、美和创造 /296

当我们本能的生活和我们在画布、大理石或文字上的努力工作之间存在一道鸿沟时,艺术就仅仅成了我们想要逃避自己真实模样的肤浅欲望的表达。

CHAPTER V

THE SCHOOL /196

Most of us want large schools with imposing buildings, even though they are obviously not the right kind of educational centres.

CHAPTER VI

PARENTS AND TEACHERS /236

The problem, therefore, is not the child, but the parent and the teacher; the problem is to educate the educator.

CHAPTER VII

SEX AND MARRIAGE /280

Sex is of the mind, and that which is of the mind must fulfil itself or there is frustration.

CHAPTER VIII

ART, BEAUTY AND CREATION /296

When there is a gap between our instinctual life and our efforts on canvas, in marble or in words, then art becomes merely an expression of our superficial desire to escape from the reality of what is.

第 一 章

教育与生活的意义

CHAPTER I

EDUCATION AND THE SIGNIFICANCE OF LIFE

当一个人周游世界时,他会注意到,不管是在印度还是美国、欧洲还是澳洲,人性是何等的相似。在高等院校中,这一点尤为明显。我们就像是在用模子生产同一种类型的人——这类人主要的兴趣就是找到安全感,成为某号重要人物,或者尽可能不做思考地及时行乐。

传统的教育使独立思考变得极为困难。遵从导致了平庸。而只要我们还在崇拜成功,想要与众不同或反抗环境就不会那么容易,并且常常会伴有风险。想要成功的强烈欲望——也就是追求物质上或所谓精神上的回报,寻找内在或外在的安全感,渴望舒适安逸——这整个过程抑制了我们的不满之情,摧毁了自发性并滋生了恐惧;而恐惧则阻碍了我们智慧地去了解生活。于是,随着年龄的增加,头脑和心灵就开始变得迟钝了。

在寻求舒适安逸的过程中,我们通常都会在生活中找到一处冲突最少的僻静角落,然后我们害怕跨出这个隐蔽之所。这种对生活的恐惧,对困难和新体验的恐惧,扼杀了我们内心的冒险精神;我们所受的一切培养和教育,都让我们害怕自己会变得和邻居不一样,害怕自己的想法会与社会的既定模式背道而驰,它使我们错误地去尊崇权威和传统。

When one travels around the world, one notices to what an degree human nature is the same, whether in India or America, in Europe or Australia. This is especially true in colleges and universities. We are turning out, as if through a mould, a type of human being whose chief interest is to find security, to become somebody important, or to have a good time with as little thought as possible.

Conventional education makes independent thinking extremely difficult. Conformity leads to mediocrity. To be different from the group or to resist environment is not easy and is often risky as long as we worship success. The urge to be successful, which is the pursuit of reward whether in the material or in the so-called spiritual sphere, the search for inward or outward security, the desire for comfort — this whole process smothers discontent, puts an end to spontaneity and breeds fear; and fear blocks the intelligent understanding of life. With increasing age, dullness of mind and heart sets in.

In seeking comfort, we generally find a quiet corner in life where there is a minimum of conflict, and then we are afraid to step out of that seclusion. This fear of life, this fear of struggle and of new experience, kills in us the spirit of adventure; our whole upbringing and education have made us afraid to be different from our neighbour, afraid to think contrary to the established pattern of society, falsely respectful of authority and tradition.

幸运的是，还是有少数认真的人，他们愿意摒弃左派或右派的偏见，去检视我们人类的问题；然而，我们绝大多数人的心中并没有真正的不满之情和反抗精神。当我们在缺乏了解的情况下屈从于环境之后，任何我们也许曾经有过的反抗精神都逐渐平息了下来，过了没多久，我们身上的各种责任便让这种反抗精神消失殆尽了。

有两种反抗：一种是暴力的反抗——那只不过是一种被动反应，在毫无了解的情况下，去对抗现有的秩序；还有一种是由智慧而生的、深层的心理反抗。很多人反抗既定的正统观念，却不料自己只是落入了新的正统观念、更深的幻想和巧加隐藏的自我放纵而已。通常的情况就是，我们脱离了某个团体或某套理想，然后又加入了另外的团体，接受了其他的理想，从而又制造出了新的思想模式，然后我们将不得不再次去反抗这套模式。反应只会造成对立，改革以后还需要进一步的改革。

然而有一种充满智慧的反抗，它不是一种被动反应，而是通过觉察自己的思想和感受，伴随着从中产生的自我了解而出现的。只有在经验来临时，我们去面对它，不回避那些烦扰，我们才能保持智慧的高度觉醒；而高度觉醒的智慧就是直觉，直觉才是生活中唯一真正的向导。

Fortunately, there are a few who are in earnest, who are willing to examine our human problems without the prejudice of the right left; but in the vast majority of us, there is no real spirit of discontent, of revolt. When we yield uncomprehendingly to environment, any spirit of revolt that we may have had dies down, and our responsibilities soon put an end to it.

Revolt is of two kinds: there is violent revolt, which is mere reaction, without understanding, against the existing order; and there is the deep psychological revolt of intelligence. There are many who revolt against the established orthodoxies only to fall into new orthodoxies, further illusions and concealed self-indulgences. What generally happens is that we break away from one group or set of ideals and join another group, take up other ideals, thus creating a new pattern of thought against which we will again have to revolt. Reaction only breeds opposition, and reform needs further reform.

But there is an intelligent revolt which is not reaction, and which comes with self-knowledge through the awareness of one's own thought and feeling. It is only when we face experience as it comes and do not avoid disturbance that we keep intelligence highly awakened; and intelligence highly awakened is intuition, which is the only true guide in life.

那么，生活的意义是什么？我们活着是为了什么？我们奋斗又是为了什么呢？如果我们接受教育只是为了功成名就，找到一份更好的工作，变得更有效率，能够使唤更多的人，那么我们的生活就会变得肤浅而空洞。如果我们接受教育只是为了成为科学家，成为只会啃书本的学者或者沉溺于知识的专家，那么我们将给世界带来不幸，甚至会将世界推向毁灭。

虽然生活的确有着一种更高、更广阔的意义，可如果我们从未发现这种意义，我们的教育又有什么价值呢？我们也许受过高等教育，但如果我们的思想和情感不能深刻地融为一体，我们的生活就是不完整的、矛盾的、被无数恐惧撕裂的；只要教育还没有培养出一种整体性的人生观，它就没有多大意义。

在如今的文明世界里，我们已经把生活分成了如此之多的部分，以至于教育除了能让我们学习一门特定技术或职业技能之外，便没有多大意义了。教育并没有唤醒个体完整的智慧，反而鼓励他去遵从某种模式，由此便妨碍了他把自己作为一个整体性的过程加以了解。试图在每个问题各自的层面、分门别类地去解决生活中的诸多问题——这表明了我们完全缺乏了解。

Now, what is the significance of life? What are we living and struggling for? If we are being educated merely to achieve distinction, to get a better job, to be more efficient, to have wider domination over others, then our lives will be shallow and empty. If we are being educated only to be scientists, to be scholars wedded to books, or specialists addicted to knowledge, then we shall be contributing to the destruction and misery of the world.

Though there is a higher and wider significance to life, of what value is our education if we never discover it? We may be highly educated, but if we are without deep integration of thought and feeling, our lives are incomplete, contradictory and torn with many fears; and as long as education does not cultivate an integrated outlook on life, it has very little significance.

In our present civilization we have divided life into so many departments that education has very little meaning, except in learning a particular technique or profession. Instead of awakening the integrated intelligence of the individual, education is encouraging him to conform to a pattern and so is hindering his comprehension of himself as a total process. To attempt to solve the many problems of existence at their respective levels, separated as they are into various categories, indicates an utter lack of comprehension.

个体是由不同的存在部分所组成的，然而强调它们的差异，并且鼓励发展某个特定类型的部分，就会导致诸多的复杂与矛盾。教育应该使这些分离的存在部分融为一体，因为如果不融为一体，生活就会变成一连串的冲突和悲伤。如果我们的诉讼永无休止，那么把我们培养成律师又有什么用？如果我们还是继续困惑，那么知识又有什么价值？如果科技和工业的力量只是被我们用来摧毁彼此的话，它们的意义又何在？如果我们的生活带来的是暴力和彻底的不幸，那它又有什么意义？虽然我们也许很有钱或者有能力赚钱，虽然我们有着自己的快乐和组织化的宗教，但我们依然活在无止境的冲突中。

我们必须分清个人与个体。个人是一种偶然性；我所说的偶然性指的是出生的背景，我们凑巧在其中生活长大的环境，以及那个环境所包含的民族主义、迷信、阶级区分和偏见。个人或偶然性只是短暂的片刻，虽然这个短暂的片刻也许会持续一生的时间；由于如今的教育体系是建立在个人、偶然性和短暂之上的，所以它导致了思想的扭曲反常，并且灌输了自我防卫性的恐惧。

The individual is made up of different entities, but to emphasize the differences and to encourage the development of a definite type leads to many complexities and contradictions. Education should bring about the integration of these separate entities — for without integration, life becomes a series of conflicts and sorrows. Of what value is it to be trained as lawyers if we perpetuate litigation? Of what value is knowledge if we continue in our confusion? What significance has technical and industrial capacity if we use it to destroy one another? What is the point of our existence if it leads to violence and utter misery? Though we may have money or are capable of earning it, though we have our pleasures and our organized religions, we are in endless conflict.

We must distinguish between the personal and the individual. Thepersonal is the accidental; and by the accidental I mean the circumstances of birth, the environment in which we happen to have been brought up, with its nationalism, superstitions, class distinctions and prejudices. The personal or accidental is but momentary, though that moment may last a lifetime; and as the present system of education is based on the personal, the accidental, the momentary, it leads to perversion of thought and the inculcation of self-defensive fears.

我们所有人一直都被教育、被环境训练着去寻求一己私利和安全感，去为自己奋斗。虽然我们用各种动听的言辞来掩盖它，然而我们都是在这个体系中接受教育——这个体系建立在剥削和因贪婪而生的恐惧之上——然后去从事各种职业的。而这种训练不可避免地会给我们和这个世界带来混乱与不幸，因为它在每个人心中制造了心理上的屏障，这种屏障把他和其他人分离开来，并维持这种分离、孤立的状态。

教育不仅仅是训练头脑。训练提升了效率，却没有造就人的完整。一个仅仅接受训练的头脑只是过去的延续，这样的头脑永远无法发现新事物。所以，要发现什么是正确的教育，我们必须探寻生活的全部意义。

对我们大多数人而言，完整生活的意义并不是头等重要的事，我们的教育强调那些次要的价值，只是让我们变得精通知识的某个分支。虽然知识和效率是必需的，但首要强调这些东西只会带来冲突与混乱。

All of us have been trained by education and environment to seek personal gain and security, and to fight for ourselves. Though we cover it over with pleasant phrases, we have been educated for various professions within a system which is based on exploitation and acquisitive fear. Such a training must inevitably bring confusion and misery to ourselves and to the world, for it creates in each individual those psychological barriers which separate and hold him apart from others.

Education is not merely a matter of training the mind. Training makes for efficiency, but it does not bring about completeness. A mind that has merely been trained is the continuation of the past, and such a mind can never discover the new. That is why, to find out what is right education, we will have to inquire into the whole significance of living.

To most of us, the meaning of life as a whole is not of primary importance, and our education emphasizes secondary values, merely making us proficient in some branch of knowledge. Though knowledge and efficiency are necessary, to lay chief emphasis on them only leads to conflict and confusion.

有一种由爱激发的效率,它远远超越了野心带来的效率,也更为强大;然而如果没有爱——爱才能带来对于生活的完整了解——效率只会滋生出残忍无情。这难道不是全世界实际正在发生的事吗?我们现在的教育是与工业化和战争相配套的,它以发展效率为首要目标;而我们则陷入了这个残酷竞争和彼此摧毁的机器中。如果教育导致了战争,如果它教导我们去毁灭或被毁灭,它难道不就已经彻底失败了吗?

要带来正确的教育,很显然,我们必须了解生命这个整体的意义所在,为此,我们必须有能力去思考,不是墨守成规的思考,而是直接的、真正的思考。一个墨守成规的思考者是一个没有思想的人,因为他遵循某种模式;他重复那些词句,在窠臼中思考。我们是无法抽象地或者依靠理论去了解生活的。了解生活就是了解我们自己,这既是教育的起点,也是教育的终点。

教育不仅仅是获取知识,收集各种事实数据然后把它们关联起来;教育是看到生活作为一个整体的意义所在。但整体是无法通过部分来逐渐达到的——可这就是各国政府、宗教组织和政党在试图做的事。

There is an efficiency inspired by love which goes far beyond and is much greater than the efficiency of ambition; and without love, which brings an integrated understanding of life, efficiency breeds ruthlessness. Is this not what is actually taking place all over the world? Our present education is geared to industrialization and war, its principal aim being to develop efficiency; and we are caught in this machine of ruthless competition and mutual destruction. If education leads to war, if it teaches us to destroy or be destroyed, has it not utterly failed?

To bring about right education, we must obviously understand the meaning of life as a whole, and for that we have to be able to think, not consistently, but directly and truly. A consistent thinker is a thoughtless person, because he conforms to a pattern; he repeats phrases and thinks in a groove. We cannot understand existence abstractly or theoretically. To understand life is to understand ourselves, and that is both the beginning and the end of education.

Education is not merely acquiring knowledge, gathering and correlating facts; it is to see the significance of life as a whole. But the whole cannot be approached through the part — which is what governments, organized religions and parties are attempting to do.

教育的职责是创造出完整从而智慧的人。我们或许能拿到学位，并且拥有机器般的效率，然而没有智慧。智慧不仅仅是知识；它并非来自书本，也不是由狡猾的自卫反应和激进强横的主张构成的。一个没读过书的人也许要比一个博学的人更具智慧。我们已经把考试和学位作为评判智慧的标准，并且发展出了逃避人类重大问题的狡猾头脑。智慧就是有能力洞察本质、洞察"真实现状"，而教育就是唤醒自己和他人身上的这种能力。

教育应当帮助我们发现永恒不灭的价值，这样我们就不会仅仅依赖于公式或者重复口号；它应当帮助我们拆除国家与社会的藩篱，而不是强调它们，因为正是它们造成了人与人之间的对立。不幸的是，如今的教育体系正在让我们变得顺从、机械化，严重缺乏思考；虽然它唤醒了我们的智性，却让我们的内在变得不完整、愚钝并且毫无创造性。

没有对于生活整体性的了解，我们个人和集体的问题只会不断加深和扩大。教育的目的并不只是制造出一些学者、技术人员和求职者，而是培养出摆脱了恐惧的完整的男男女女；因为只有在这些人中，才会有持久的和平。

The function of education is to create human beings who are integrated and therefore intelligent. We may take degrees and be mechanically efficient without being intelligent. Intelligence is not mere information; it is not derived from books, nor does it consist of clever self-defensive responses and aggressive assertions. One who has not studied may be more intelligent than the learned. We have made examinations and degrees the criterion of intelligence and have developed cunning minds that avoid vital human issues. Intelligence is the capacity to perceive the essential, the what is ; and to awaken this capacity, in oneself and in others, is education.

Education should help us to discover lasting values so that we do not merely cling to formulas or repeat slogans; it should help us to break down our national and social barriers, instead of emphasizing them, for they breed antagonism between man and man. Unfortunately, the present system of education is making us subservient, mechanical and deeply thoughtless; though it awakens us intellectually, inwardly it leaves us incomplete, stultified and uncreative.

Without an integrated understanding of life, our individual and collective problems will only deepen and extend. The purpose of education is not to produce mere scholars, technicians and job hunters, but integrated men and women who are free of fear; for only between such human beings can there be enduring peace.

在自我了解中，恐惧就会结束。如果一个人要每时每刻都努力应对生活，如果他要面对生活的错综复杂、无数痛苦和突如其来的需求，他就必须无比柔韧，进而摆脱掉各种理论和特定的思维模式。

教育不应该鼓励个体去遵从这个社会，或者消极地与之和谐共处，而是应该帮助他去发现伴随着毫无偏见的探究与自我觉察而出现的真正的价值。如果没有了自我了解，自我表达就会变成自负，各种富有侵略性和野心勃勃的冲突也会随之而来。教育应当唤醒人们自我觉察的能力，而不只是让人沉湎于令人满足的自我表达中。

如果我们在生活的过程中摧毁着自己，那么知识学问又有什么用？因为我们正在遭受一系列毁灭性的战争，战争一场接一场地爆发，因此我们培养孩子的方式很显然存在某种根本性的错误。我认为我们大多数人都意识到了这一点，但我们不知道如何去处理它。

不管是教育体系还是政治体系，都不会天方夜谭般地改变；只有当我们内心有了根本性的转变，它们才会有所改变。个体才是最重要的，而不是体系；只要个体还没有了解他自己整体的运作过程，就没有任何体系——不管是左派还是右派——可以给这个世界带来和平与秩序。

It is in the understanding of ourselves that fear comes to an individual is to grapple with life from moment to moment, if he is to face its intricacies, its miseries and sudden demands, he must be infinitely pliable and therefore free of theories and particular patterns of thought.

Education should not encourage the individual to conform to society or to be negatively harmonious with it, but help him to discover the true values which come with unbiased investigation and self-awareness. When there is no self-knowledge, self-expression becomes self-assertion, with all its aggressive and ambitious conflicts. Education should awaken the capacity to be self-aware and not merely indulge in gratifying self-expression.

What is the good of learning if in the process of living we are destroying ourselves? As we are having a series of devastating wars, one right after another, there is obviously something radically wrong with the way we bring up our children. I think most of us are aware of this, but we do not know how to deal with it.

Systems, whether educational or political, are not changed mysteriously; they are transformed when there is a fundamental change in ourselves. The individual is of first importance, not the system; and as long as the individual does not understand the total process of himself, no system, whether of the left or of the right, can bring order and peace to the world.

第二章

正确的教育

CHAPTER II
THE RIGHT KIND OF EDUCATION

无知之人并不是没有学问的人，而是不了解自己的人。当一个博学之人要依靠书本、知识和权威来了解事物时，他便是愚蠢的。了解只能通过自知而来，自知就是去觉察自己全部的心理过程。因此真正意义上的教育乃是对我们自身的了解，因为人类的全部存在就浓缩在我们每一个人的心里。

我们如今的所谓教育，是通过书本来积累信息和知识——这是任何识字的人都可以做的事。这种教育提供了一种微妙的逃避自我的方式，然而就像所有的逃避方式一样，它不可避免地会制造出越来越多的痛苦。冲突与混乱的产生源于我们与他人、事物和理念的错误关系，除非我们了解那种关系并改变它，否则，仅仅是学习、收集各类事实数据，获取各项技能，只会把我们带向将会吞噬一切的混乱与毁灭。

依照当今社会的"安排"，我们会把子女送去学校，让他们学一点技术以便日后可以靠它来混口饭吃。我们想让孩子首先成为一个专家，希望由此使他获得经济上的保障。可是技术的培训能使我们了解自己吗？

The ignorant man is not the unlearned, but he who does not know himself, and the learned man is stupid when he relies on books, on knowledge and on authority to give him understanding. Understanding comes only through self-knowledge, which is awareness of one's total psychological process. Thus education, in the true sense, is the understanding of oneself, for it is within each one of us that the whole of existence is gathered.

What we now call education is a matter of accumulating and knowledge from books, which anyone can do who can read. education offers a subtle form of escape from ourselves and, like all escapes, it inevitably creates increasing misery. Conflict and confusion result from our own wrong relationship with people, things and ideas, and until we understand that relationship and alter it, mere learning, the gathering of facts and the acquiring of various skills, can only lead us to engulfing chaos and destruction.

As society is now organized, we send our children to school to learn some technique by which they can eventually earn a livelihood. We want to make the child first and foremost a specialist, hoping thus to give him a secure economic position. But does the cultivation of a technique enable us to understand ourselves?

显而易见，我们必须懂得如何读书写字，需要学习工程学或者其他专业，但技术能赋予我们了解生活的能力吗？毫无疑问，技术是次要的；如果技术成了我们唯一奋力争取的事物，我们很显然就否定了生命中更为伟大的部分。

生活就是痛苦、喜悦、美丽、丑陋和爱，当我们把它作为一个整体，从每一个层面去了解它，这种了解就会创造出它自己的技术。但反过来就不对了：技术永远无法带来创造性的了解。

如今的教育过分强调了技术。在对技术的过分强调中，我们摧毁了人类。在不了解生活，也没有广泛、全面地觉察到思想和欲望的运作方式的情况下去培养能力和效率只会使我们愈发无情，而这又会引起战争，从而危及我们的人身安全。专门的技术培训生产出了科学家、数学家、桥梁工程师、太空征服者，可这些人了解生活的整个过程吗？有哪个专家能够完整地去体验生活？只有当他不是专家时，这才成为可能。

While it is obviously necessary to know how to read and write, and to learn engineering or some other profession, will technique give us the capacity to understand life? Surely, technique is secondary; and if technique is the only thing we are striving for, we are obviously denying what is by far the greater part of life.

Life is pain, joy, beauty, ugliness, love, and when we understand it as a whole, at every level, that understanding creates its own technique. But the contrary is not true: technique can never bring about creative understanding.

Present-day education has overemphasized technique. In overemphasizing technique we destroy man. To cultivate capacity and efficiency without understanding life, without having a comprehensive perception of the ways of thought and desire, will only make us increasingly ruthless, which is to engender wars and jeopardize our physical security. The exclusive cultivation of technique has produced scientists, mathematicians, bridge builders, space conquerors; but do they understand the total process of life? Can any specialist experience life as a whole? Only when he ceases to be a specialist.

科学技术的进步在某种层面上确实为一些人解决了某些问题，然而，它也引发了更广、更深层的问题。仅仅生活于某个层面而忽视生活的整体过程，将会招致不幸与毁灭。每个人最大的需求和最迫切的问题，就是要有一种对生活的完整了解——这种了解将使他有能力面对生活中日益增长的错综复杂。

技术知识——不管它有多么必要——绝不可能解决我们内在和心理上的压力与冲突。正因为我们获得了技术知识却不了解生活的整体过程，才导致技术变成了毁灭自我的手段。一个知道如何分裂原子但内心没有爱的人，就会变成一个恶魔。

我们根据自己的能力选择了一种职业，但从事一项职业就能带领我们走出冲突与混乱吗？某种技术培训似乎是必需的，然而即使我们成了工程师、内科医生、会计，那又能怎样呢？从事某项职业就是生命的圆满吗？很显然，我们大部分人就是这样认为的。我们所从事的各种职业或许能使我们一生中的大部分时间都保持忙碌；然而，我们所制造的并且如此为之着迷的那些东西本身，却导致了毁灭与不幸。我们的态度和价值观，使得那些东西和职业变成了嫉妒、痛苦和仇恨的工具。

Technological progress does solve certain kinds of problems for people at one level, but it introduces wider and deeper issues too. at one level, disregarding the total process of life, is to invite misery and destruction. The greatest need and most pressing problem for every individual is to have an integrated comprehension of life, which will enable him to meet its ever-increasing complexities.

Technical knowledge, however necessary, will in no way inner, psychological pressures and conflicts; and it is because acquired technical knowledge without understanding the total process of life that technology has become a means of destroying ourselves. The man who knows how to split the atom but has no love in his heart becomes a monster.

We choose a vocation according to our capacities; but will the following of a vocation lead us out of conflict and confusion? Some form of technical training seems necessary; but when we have become engineers, physicians, accountants — then what? Is the practice of a profession the fulfilment of life? Apparently with most of us it is. Our various professions may keep us busy for the greater part of our existence; but the very things that we produce and are so entranced with are causing destruction and misery. Our attitudes and values make of things and occupations the instruments of envy, bitterness and hate.

仅仅从事某项职业，却不了解我们自己，就会导致挫败感，而我们不可避免地会通过各种有害的活动来逃避这种挫败感。拥有技术却没有了解，就会导致仇恨和残忍，而我们却用动听的词句来掩盖它。如果强调技术、成为高效率的个体所带来的结果是彼此毁灭，那么这一切又有什么价值？

当职业的重要性凌驾于一切之上时，生活就会变得无聊、沉闷、令人厌倦，成为一种机械和枯燥的例行公事，于是我们通过各种娱乐消遣来逃避它。积累事实数据和培养技能——我们把这称为教育——剥夺了我们完整生活与行动的丰盈、充实。正因为我们不了解生活的整体过程，我们才会紧握住能力和效率不放，由此它们便具有了压倒性的重要性。我们是无法通过"部分"来了解整体的，只有通过行动和体验，我们才能了解整体。

Without understanding ourselves, mere occupation leads to frustration, with its inevitable escapes through all kinds of mischievous activities. Technique without understanding leads to enmity and ruthlessness, which we cover up with pleasant-sounding phrases. Of what value is it to emphasize technique and become efficient entities if the result is mutual destruction?

When function is all-important, life becomes dull and boring, a mechanical and sterile routine from which we escape into every kind of distraction. The accumulation of facts and the development of capacity, which we call education, has deprived us of the fullness of integrated life and action. It is because we do not understand the total process of life that we cling to capacity and efficiency, which thus assume overwhelming importance. But the whole cannot be understood through the part; it can be understood only through action and experience.

培养技能的另一个因素是它给了我们一种安全感，不仅是经济上的安全感，还包括心理上的安全感。知道自己有能力而且效率高，这让人感到安心。知道自己会弹钢琴、会造房子，这带给我们一种充满活力的感觉和咄咄逼人的独立性。然而，出于渴望心理上的安全感而去强调才能，就否定了生活的丰富性和完整性。生活的全部内容永远无法预知，我们必须一刻接一刻地重新体验它；可因为我们害怕未知的事物，于是我们就以体系、技能和信仰的形式，为自己建立起了心理上的安全地带。只要我们还在寻求内心的安全感，我们就不可能了解生活的全部过程。

正确的教育，在它鼓励人们学习某项技能的同时，也应当实现某种更为重要的价值：它应该帮助人类去体验生活的完整过程。这种体验将会把能力和技术放到它们正确的位置上。如果一个人真的有话要说，那么这些肺腑之言本身就会创造出它自己的演说风格；然而学习某种演说风格而没有内在的体验，就只会导致肤浅。

Another factor in the cultivation of technique is that it gives us a sense of security, not only economic, but psychological as well. It is reassuring to know that we are capable and efficient. To know that we can play the piano or build a house gives us a feeling of vitality, of aggressive independence; but to emphasize capacity because of a desire for psychological security is to deny the fullness of life. The whole content of life can never be foreseen, it must be experienced anew from moment to moment; but we are afraid of the unknown, and so we establish for ourselves psychological zones of safety in the form of systems, techniques and beliefs. As long as we are seeking inward security, the total process of life cannot be understood.

The right kind of education, while encouraging the learning of a technique, should accomplish something which is of far greater importance: it should help man to experience the integrated process of life. It is this experiencing that will put capacity and technique in their right place. If one really has something to say, the very saying of it creates its own style; but learning a style without inward experiencing can only lead to superficiality.

全世界的工程师都在疯狂地设计各种无须人类操作的机器。在这种几乎完全是靠机器来推动运行的生活里，人类又会变成什么样？我们会有越来越多的闲暇时间，却不知道如何明智地利用它，于是，我们便通过知识、通过使人精疲力竭的娱乐或者各种理想来寻求逃避。

我相信已经有无数关于教育理想的书籍，然而我们比以往任何时候都更加困惑。教育一个孩子，使其变得完整和自由是没有方法可循的。只要我们还在关心原则、理想和方法，我们就没有帮助个体摆脱他自我中心的活动及其所有的恐惧和冲突。

完美乌托邦的理想和蓝图，永远不会带来心灵的彻底改变，然而要结束战争和遍及世界的毁灭，心灵的彻底改变是不可或缺的。理想无法改变我们现有的价值观念，只有通过正确的教育——也就是培养对于真实现状的了解——才能改变它们。

Throughout the world, engineers are frantically designing machines which do not need men to operate them. In a life run almost entirely by machines, what is to become of human beings? We shall have more and more leisure without knowing wisely how to employ it, and we shall seek escape through knowledge, through enfeebling amusements, or through ideals.

I believe volumes have been written about educational ideals, yet we are in greater confusion than ever before. There is no method by which to educate a child to be integrated and free. As long as we are concerned with principles, ideals and methods, we are not helping the individual to be free from his own self-centred activity with all its fears and conflicts.

Ideals and blueprints for a perfect Utopia will never bring about the radical change of heart which is essential if there is to be an end to war and universal destruction. Ideals cannot change our present values: they can be changed only by the right kind of education, which is to foster the understanding of what is.

当我们齐心协力为了理想和未来工作时，我们就会根据我们对未来的设想来塑造个体；我们根本不关心人类，我们关心的是"我们认为他们应该怎样"的想法。对我们来说，应该怎样已经变得远远比人的实际情况——也就是个体及其错综复杂的问题——更加重要。如果我们可以开始直接去了解个体，而不是通过我们认为"他应该怎样"的屏障去观察他，那么我们关注的就是真实现状。那时我们就不会再想要把个体改造成其他人了，我们唯一关心的是帮助他了解自己——在这之中是没有个人的动机或利益的。如果我们充分地觉察到真实现状，我们就可以理解它，从而摆脱它；然而，要觉察到真实的自己，我们就必须停止那种努力去"成为别人"的奋斗。

教育中没有理想的一席之地，因为理想阻碍了对"现在"的了解。毫无疑问，只有当我们不逃避到未来中去，我们才能觉察到真实现状。期盼未来，奋力追求理想，表明了心灵的怠惰，以及想要逃避"现在"的渴望。

When we are working together for an ideal, for the future, we individuals according to our conception of that future; we are not concerned with human beings at all, but with our idea of what they should be. The what should be becomes far more important to us than what is, namely, the individual with his complexities. If we begin to understand the individual directly instead of looking at him through the screen of what we think he should be, then we are concerned with what is. Then we no longer want to transform the individual into something else; our only concern is to help him to understand himself, and in this there is no personal motive or gain. If we are fully aware of what is, we shall understand it and so be free of it; but to be aware of what we are, we must stop struggling after something which we are not.

Ideals have no place in education for they prevent the comprehension of the present. Surely, we can be aware of what is only when we do not escape into the future. To look to the future, to strain after an ideal, indicates sluggishness of mind and a desire to avoid the present.

追求一个现成的乌托邦不就否定了个体的自由与完整吗?当某人追随一个理想、一种模式时,当某人有了一个"应该怎样"的公式时,他难道不是在过着一种非常肤浅和机械化的生活吗?我们需要的不是理想主义者或者带着机械化头脑的存在体,而是拥有智慧和自由的完整的人。仅仅去设计一个完美的社会,我们就会为了"应该怎样"而争论不休、流血牺牲,与此同时却忽视了我们的真实现状。

如果人类是机械化的存在体,是无意识的机器,那么未来就是可以预知的,而我们也可以描绘出关于完美乌托邦的计划;那时我们就能够精心设计一个未来的社会并且为之努力奋斗。然而,人类并不是根据某个特定模板制造出来的机器。

"现在"和"未来"之间横亘着一道巨大的鸿沟,其间有着无数的影响在作用于我们每一个人。当我们为了未来而牺牲现在时,我们就是在追求通过错误的手段来达到一个可能正确的结果。然而,手段决定了结果;何况,我们是何许人也,竟能决定人类"应该怎样"?我们又有什么权力依据某种特定的模式——从书本中学到的模式或者由我们自己的野心、希望和恐惧设定的模式——来试图塑造人类呢?

Is not the pursuit of a ready-made Utopia a denial of the integration of the individual? When one follows an ideal, a one has a formula for what should be, does one not live a very superficial, automatic life? We need, not idealists or entities with mechanical minds, but integrated human beings who are intelligent and free. Merely to have a design for a perfect society is to wrangle and shed blood for what should be while ignoring what is.

If human beings were mechanical entities, automatic machines, then the future would be predictable and the plans for a perfect Utopia could be drawn up; then we would be able to plan carefully a future society and work towards it. But human beings are not machines to be established according to a definite pattern.

Between now and the future there is an immense gap in which many influences are at work upon each one of us, and in sacrificing the present for the future we are pursuing wrong means to a probable right end. But the means determine the end; and besides, who are we to decide what man should be? By what right do we seek to mould him according to a particular pattern, learnt from some book or determined by our own ambitions, hopes and fears?

正确的教育并不是建立在任何体系上的——不管是多么精心构想的体系;它也不是以某种特殊方式来制约个体的手段。真正意义上的教育是帮助个体变得成熟和自由,使其在爱和良善中尽情绽放。这才是我们应该关心的,而不是根据某个理想化的模板来塑造孩子。

任何根据性格和天资对孩子进行归类的方法,都只强调了他们之间的差异,它造成了对立,助长了社会的分裂,从而无助于培养出完整的人。很显然,没有任何方法或体系可以提供正确的教育,而恪守某一特定的教育方法则表明了教育者的怠惰。只要教育还是建立在呆板的原则之上,它便可以生产出高效率的男男女女,然而无法培养出具有创造性的人。

只有爱才能使我们理解别人。当有了爱,我们就能立即与他人产生同一时间、同一层次上的交流。

The right kind of education is not based on any system, however carefully thought out; nor is it a means of conditioning the individual in some special manner. Education in the true sense is helping the individual to be mature and free, to flower greatly in love and goodness. That is what we should be interested in, and not in shaping the child according to some idealistic pattern.

Any method which classifies children according to aptitude merely emphasizes their differences; it breeds antagonism, encourages divisions in society and does not help to develop integrated human beings. It is obvious that no method or system can provide the right kind of education, and strict adherence to a particular method indicates sluggishness on the part of the educator. As long as education is based on cut-and-dried principles, it can turn out men and women who are efficient, but it cannot produce creative human beings.

Only love can bring about the understanding of another. Where there is love there is instantaneous communion with the other, on the same level and at the same time.

我们无法让生活去顺应某种体系,也无法强迫它进入到某个框架里——不管那个框架被构想得如何高尚;一个仅仅被培养着去掌握事实性知识的头脑,是无法面对生活及其所有的多变、微妙、深度和惊人的高度的。当我们根据某种思想体系,或者一套特定的规章制度来训练我们的孩子时,当我们教导他们在各个分离的部门中思考时,我们便阻碍了他们成长为完整的男女的进程,由此他们便无法智慧地去思考——也就是去面对生活这个整体了。

教育的最高职责在于培养出一个完整的人——他能够把生活作为一个整体加以处理。而理想主义者就像那些专家一样,他们关心的不是整体,而只是某一部分。只要我们还在追求一种理想的行动模式,就不可能有完整;而很多老师都是理想主义者,他们已经扔掉了爱,他们头脑干涸、内心冷酷。为了研究孩子,我们必须警觉、留心和自知,而比起鼓励孩子去跟从某个理想,这需要更为深厚的智慧和关爱。

Life cannot be made to conform to a system, it cannot be forced into a framework, however nobly conceived; and a mind that has merely been trained in factual knowledge is incapable of meeting life with its variety, its subtlety, its depths and great heights. When we train our children according to a system of thought or a particular discipline, when we teach them to think within departmental divisions, we prevent them from growing into integrated men and women, and therefore they are incapable of thinking intelligently, which is to meet life as a whole.

The highest function of education is to bring about an integrated individual who is capable of dealing with life as a whole. The idealist, like the specialist, is not concerned with the whole, but only with a part. There can be no integration as long as one is pursuing an ideal pattern of action; and some teachers who are idealists have put away love, they have dry minds and hard hearts. To study a child, one has to be alert, watchful, self-aware, and this demands far greater intelligence and affection than to encourage him to follow an ideal.

教育的另一个职责，是创造新的价值。仅仅把现存的价值灌输到小孩的头脑中，让他去遵从某些理想，这就束缚了他，而没有唤醒他的智慧。教育和当今世界的危机密切相关，而一个看到了这种遍及世界的混乱起因何在的教育者，应该问问自己：要怎样唤醒学生心中的智慧，从而帮助下一代人不再制造进一步的冲突和灾难？他必须倾注自己所有的思考、关心和爱来创造出一个恰当的环境，来培育孩子内心的智慧，因此当小孩长大成人以后，他就能智慧地去处理他所面临的人类问题。但要做到这一点，教育者就必须了解他自己，而不是依赖于体系和信仰。

Another function of education is to create new values. Merely to implant existing values in the mind of the child, to make him conform to ideals, is to condition him without awakening his intelligence. Education is intimately related to the present world crisis, and the educator who sees the causes of this universal chaos should ask himself how to awaken intelligence in the student, thus helping the coming generation not to bring about further conflict and disaster. He must give all his thought, all his care and affection to the creation of right environment and to the development of understanding, so that when the child grows into maturity he will be capable of dealing intelligently with the human problems that confront him. But in order to do this, the educator must understand himself instead of relying on systems and beliefs.

让我们不要依照原则和理想去思考，而是去关心事物的真实模样；因为正是对于真实现状的深刻思考唤醒了智慧，而教育者自身的智慧远远要比他知道某种新的教育方法更加重要。当某人遵循某种方法时——即使这个方法是由深思熟虑和聪慧的人所设计出来的——方法本身也会变得非常重要，而孩子只有适合这种方法时，才会显得重要。我们评估孩子，把他们加以分类，然后开始依照分类图表来对他进行教育。这种教育流程对老师来说或许很便利，然而，不管是实行某种教育体系，还是专横地对待学生的观念和学习态度，都无法带来一个完整的人。

正确的教育在于如实地了解孩子，而不是把我们认为"他应该怎样"的理想强加在他身上。把孩子纳入理想的框架，就是在鼓励他去遵从——这滋生了恐惧，并且在他内心制造出了他的真实模样和他"应该怎样"之间的持续冲突；而所有内在的冲突，都会从外在表现于社会中。理想是一个真实的障碍，它阻碍了我们了解孩子，也阻碍了孩子了解他自己。

Let us not think in terms of principles and ideals, but be with things as they are; for it is the consideration of what is that intelligence, and the intelligence of the educator is far more important than his knowledge of a new method of education. When one follows a method, even if it has been worked out by a thoughtful and intelligent person, the method becomes very important, and the children are important only as they fit into it. One measures and classifies the child, and then proceeds to educate him according to some chart. This process of education may be convenient for the teacher, but neither the practice of a system nor the tyranny of opinion and learning can bring about an integrated human being.

The right kind of education consists in understanding the child as he is without imposing upon him an ideal of what we think he should enclose him in the framework of an ideal is to encourage him to conform, which breeds fear and produces in him a constant conflict between what he is and what he should be; and all inward conflicts have their outward manifestations in society. Ideals are an actual hindrance to our understanding of the child and to the child's understanding of himself.

真正渴望了解自己孩子的父母,是不会透过理想的屏障来看孩子的。如果他爱孩子,他就会观察他,他会研究他的习惯、他的情绪和特质。只有当我们不爱孩子时,才会把理想强加于他,因为那时我们正试图在孩子身上实现自己的野心——想要孩子成为这个或那个。当一个人爱的不是理想而是孩子时,才有可能帮助孩子去如实了解他自己。

举个例子,如果某个小孩撒谎了,那么把"诚实"的理想放在他面前又有什么用呢?我们必须去搞清楚为什么他要撒谎。要帮助孩子,我们必须花时间去研究和观察他——这需要耐心、爱和关怀;然而当我们没有爱也没有了解时,我们便会把孩子强行纳入我们称之为"理想"的行动模式中去。

理想是一种方便的逃避,而追随理想的老师是无法了解他的学生并智慧地对待他们的;对他来说,未来的理想和"应该怎样"远远要比眼前的孩子更加重要。对理想的追求排斥了爱,而没有爱,人类的任何问题都无法得到解决。

A parent who really desires to understand his child does not look at him through the screen of an ideal. If he loves the child, he observes him, he studies his tendencies, his moods and peculiarities. It is only when one feels no love for the child that one imposes upon him an ideal, for then one's ambitions are trying to fulfil themselves in him, wanting him to become this or that. If one loves, not the ideal, but the child, then there is a possibility of helping him to understand himself as he is.

If a child tells lies, for example, of what value is it to put before him the ideal of truth? One has to find out why he is telling lies. To help the child, one has to take time to study and observe him, which demands patience, love and care; but when one has no love, no understanding, then one forces the child into a pattern of action which we call an ideal.

Ideals are a convenient escape, and the teacher who follows them is incapable of understanding his students and dealing with them intelligently; for him, the future ideal, the what should be, is far more important than the present child. The pursuit of an ideal excludes love, and without love no human problem can be solved.

正确的老师不会依赖于某种教学方法，而是会去研究每一个学生。在我们和孩子还有年轻人的相处中，我们所面对的并不是一些可以快速修好的机器，而是活生生的人——他们容易受到影响、喜怒无常、敏感、恐惧、有自己的感情；和他们打交道，我们必须要有极大的理解、耐心和爱。而当我们缺乏这些东西时，我们便会求助于快速简便的特效药，希望它能带来神奇和理所当然的效果。如果我们的态度和行为是毫无觉察的、机械化的，我们就会避开针对我们提出的任何要求——那些令人不安而又无法以惯性反应去应对的要求，而这就是我们教育中最主要的困难之一。

孩子是"过去"和"现在"两方面影响下的结果，因此他已经受到了制约。如果我们把自己的背景传递给孩子，我们就会使他的局限和我们自己的局限永远存在下去。只有当我们了解了自身的局限并且摆脱它以后，才会有根本性的转变。当我们自己还饱受制约时，去讨论"什么是正确的教育"完全是徒劳的。

If the teacher is of the right kind, he will not depend on a method, but will study each individual pupil. In our relationship with children and young people, we are not dealing with mechanical devices that can be quickly repaired, but with living beings who are impressionable, volatile, sensitive, afraid, affectionate; and to deal with them, we have to have great understanding, the strength of patience and love. When we lack these, we look to quick and easy remedies and hope for marvellous and automatic results. If we are unaware, mechanical in our attitudes and actions, we fight shy of any demand upon us that is disturbing and that cannot be met by an automatic response, and this is one of our major difficulties in education.

The child is the result of both the past and the present and is therefore already conditioned. If we transmit our background to the child, we perpetuate both his and our own conditioning. There is radical transformation only when we understand our own conditioning and are free of it. To discuss what should be the right kind of education while we ourselves are conditioned is utterly futile.

当孩子年幼时,毫无疑问我们必须保护他们免遭肉体的伤害,使他们不会有身体上的不安全感。但不幸的是,我们并未就此止步,我们还想改造他们的思维和感受的方式,我们想要依照我们自己的渴望和意图来塑造他们。我们在孩子身上寻求自我的实现,通过他们来使自己不朽。我们在他们周围竖起围墙,用我们自己的信仰和意识形态、恐惧和希望来限制他们;然后当他们在战争中牺牲或致残,或以其他方式遭受生活的痛苦折磨时,我们就会为之哭泣和祈祷。

这些经验并不能带来自由;相反,它们加强了自我的意志。自我是由一系列自卫性和扩张性的反应组成的,它总是在自身的投射和令人满意的认同中获得满足。只要我们还是依照自我、"我"和"我的"来诠释经验,只要那个"我"、那个自我还在经由自身的反应维持着自己,经验就无法摆脱冲突、困惑和痛苦。只有当一个人了解了自我和经验者的运作方式,自由才会降临。只有当自我及其积累起来的反应没有成为"经验者",经验才会呈现出一种完全不同的意义,从而成为一种创造。

While the children are young, we must of course protect them from physical harm and prevent them from feeling physically insecure. But unfortunately we do not stop there; we want to shape their ways of thinking and feeling, we want to mould them in accordance with our own cravings and intentions. We seek to fulfil ourselves in our children, to perpetuate ourselves through them. We build walls around them, condition them by our beliefs and ideologies, fears and hopes — and then we cry and pray when they are killed or maimed in wars, or otherwise made to suffer by the experiences of life.

Such experiences do not bring about freedom; on the contrary, they strengthen the will of the self. The self is made up of a series of defensive and expansive reactions, and its fulfilment is always in its own projections and gratifying identifications. As long as we translate experience in terms of the self, of the "me" and the "mine", as long as the "I", the ego, maintains itself through its reactions, experience cannot be freed from conflict, confusion and pain. Freedom comes only when one understands the ways of the self, the experiencer. It is only when the self, with its accumulated reactions, is not the experiencer, that experience takes on an entirely different significance and becomes creation.

如果我们想要帮助孩子从导致了如此多痛苦的自我运作方式中摆脱出来，我们每个人就应该着手深刻地转变自己对孩子的态度，以及和孩子的关系。父母和教育者可以通过自身的思想和行为，来帮助孩子获得自由，让他在爱和良善中绽放。

如今的教育，并没有鼓励我们去了解我们继承下来的各种倾向和环境的影响——正是这两者制约了头脑和心灵并且维持了恐惧，因此教育并没有帮助我们打破这些局限，从而成为一个完整的人。任何形式的教育——如果它关心的只是部分，而不是人的整体——它就必然会导致不断增长的冲突和痛苦。

只有在个体的自由中，爱和良善才会绽放；而唯有正确的教育才能带给我们这种自由。不管是遵从如今的社会，还是承诺一个未来的乌托邦，都永远无法给个体带来那份洞察——而没有洞察，一个人就会不断地制造问题。

If we would help the child to be free from the ways of the self, which cause so much suffering, then each one of us should set about altering deeply his attitude and relationship to the child. Parents and educators, by their own thought and conduct, can help the child to be free and to flower in love and goodness.

Education as it is at present in no way encourages the understanding of the inherited tendencies and environmental influences which condition the mind and heart and sustain fear, and therefore it does not help us to break through these conditionings and bring about an integrated human being. Any form of education that concerns itself with a part and not with the whole of man inevitably leads to increasing conflict and suffering.

It is only in individual freedom that love and goodness can flower; and the right kind of education alone can offer this freedom. Neither conformity to the present society nor the promise of a future Utopia can ever give to the individual that insight without which he is constantly creating problems.

正确的教育者，在看到了自由的内在本质后，会帮助每一个学生去观察和了解他自我投射的种种价值和各种强加于他的事物；他会帮助学生觉察到周围制约着他的各种影响，以及他自身的各种欲望——这两者都局限了他的心灵，并培育了恐惧；他会帮助学生，由此当学生长大成人后，就能在他和各种事物的关系中去观察和了解自己，因为正是渴望自我满足带来了无尽的冲突和悲伤。

毫无疑问，帮助个体洞察生活不朽的价值，并且免于任何局限，这是可能的。有人或许会说这种个体性的充分发展将会造成混乱，它会吗？这个世界已经混乱不堪了，而混乱之所以产生，是因为我们没有教育个体去了解自己。在给予了个体一些表面自由的同时，我们也教导他去顺应和接受现有的价值。

为了对抗这种严格的控制，很多人奋起反抗，但不幸的是他们的反抗仅仅是一种追求个人利益的反应，这种反抗只是让我们的生活变得更黑暗了。正确的教育者会觉察到心灵所具有的那种产生反应的倾向，然后会帮助学生去改变现有的价值——不是出于反抗它们的反应，而是通过了解生活的整体过程从而改变它。没有个体的完整——正确的教育就可以帮助唤醒这种完整——就不可能有人与人之间的充分合作。

The right kind of educator, seeing the inward nature of freedom, helps each individual student to observe and understand his own self-projected values and impositions; he helps him to become aware of the conditioning influences about him, and of his own desires, both of which limit his mind and breed fear; he helps him, as he grows to manhood, to observe and understand himself in relation to all things, for it is the craving for self- fulfilment that brings endless conflict and sorrow.

Surely, it is possible to help the individual to perceive the enduring values of life, without conditioning. Some may say that this full development of the individual will lead to chaos; but will it? There is already confusion in the world, and it has arisen because the individual has not been educated to understand himself. While he has been given some superficial freedom, he has also been taught to conform, to accept the existing values.

Against this regimentation, many are revolting; but revolt is a mere self-seeking reaction, which only further darkens our existence. The right kind of educator, aware of the mind's tendency to reaction, helps the student to alter present values, not out of reaction against them, but through understanding the total process of life. Full cooperation between man and man is not possible without the integration which right education can help to awaken in the individual.

为什么我们如此肯定地认为，不管是我们还是下一代人，都无法通过正确的教育来彻底改变人类的关系？我们从未尝试过，因为我们大多数人似乎都害怕正确的教育，所以我们不愿去尝试它。我们没有真正地去探究这整个问题，而是坚持认为人的本性是无法改变的，我们安于现状，并且鼓励孩子去适应如今的社会；我们制约他，让他顺应我们现有的生活方式，并且期望能获得最好的结果。但这种会导致战争与饥饿的对现有价值的顺应，能被认为是教育吗？

让我们不要欺骗自己，认为这种制约有助于智慧和幸福。如果我们依然恐惧、没有关爱、无可救药地冷漠，这就意味着我们其实并没有兴趣鼓励个体在爱和良善中尽情绽放，而是宁愿他继续背负着这些我们已然背负的痛苦，而他也正是这些痛苦的一部分。

对学生加以制约，让他接受如今的环境——这很显然是非常愚蠢的。除非我们能自愿地带来一次教育的彻底改变，否则我们对持续存在的混乱和不幸就负有直接的责任。当巨大且残酷的革命终于爆发时，它只是给了另一群人去剥削和变得残忍的机会。

Why are we so sure that neither we nor the coming generation, through the right kind of education, can bring about a fundamental alteration in human relationship? We have never tried it; and as most of us seem to be fearful of the right kind of education, we are disinclined to try it. Without really inquiring into this whole question, we assert that human nature cannot be changed, we accept things as they are and encourage the child to fit into the present society; we condition him to our present ways of life, and hope for the best. But can such conformity to present values, which lead to war and starvation, be considered education?

Let us not deceive ourselves that this conditioning is going to make for intelligence and happiness. If we remain fearful, devoid of affection, hopelessly apathetic, it means that we are really not interested in encouraging the individual to flower greatly in love and goodness, but prefer that he carry on the miseries with which we have burdened ourselves and of which he also is a part.

To condition the student to accept the present environment is obviously stupid. Unless we voluntarily bring about a radical education, we are directly responsible for the perpetuation of chaos and misery; and when some monstrous and brutal revolution finally comes, it will only give opportunity to another group of people to exploit and to be ruthless.

出于政治和工业上的目的，纪律已经变成如今的社会结构中的一个重要因素，正因为渴望获得心理上的安全感，所以我们才会接受和实施各种形式的纪律。纪律确保了一个结果，对我们而言，结果要比手段更重要；然而，恰恰是手段决定了结果。

纪律带来的危险之一，就是体系变得比封闭于体系中的人更加重要。于是纪律取代了爱，正因为我们内心空虚，所以才会依赖于纪律。自由是永远无法通过纪律和抵抗到来的；自由不是目标，不是一个要去达到的终点。自由在起点，而不是在终点，它无法在某个遥远的理想中找到。

自由并不意味着有了满足自我的机会，或者可以不再为他人考虑。一个认真的老师会保护孩子，用一切可能的方式去帮助他们朝着正确的自由成长；然而如果老师有任何形式的教条主义或者自私自利，他就不可能帮助学生了。

For political and industrial reasons, discipline has become an important factor in the present social structure, and it is because of our desire to be psychologically secure that we accept and practise various forms of discipline. Discipline guarantees a result, and to us the end is more important than the means; but the means determine the end.

One of the dangers of discipline is that the system becomes more important than the human beings who are enclosed in it. Discipline then becomes a substitute for love, and it is because our hearts are empty that we cling to discipline. Freedom can never come through discipline, through resistance; freedom is not a goal, an end to be achieved. Freedom is at the beginning, not at the end, it is not to be found in some distant ideal.

Freedom does not mean the opportunity for self-gratification or the setting aside of consideration for others. The teacher who is sincere will protect the children and help them in every possible way to grow towards the right kind of freedom; but it will be impossible for him to do this if he is in any way dogmatic or self-seeking.

敏感永远无法通过强迫的方式来唤醒。我们或许可以强迫孩子保持外在的安静,却没有去面对那些使孩子变得倔强、无礼等的因素。强迫滋生了对抗与恐惧。任何形式的奖励和惩罚只会让心灵变得顺从与迟钝;如果这就是我们想要的,那么这种以强制为手段的教育,便是一种可以继续下去的最好方式。

然而,这种教育既无法帮助我们了解孩子,也无法建立一个正确的、没有分裂与仇恨的社会环境。在对孩子的爱中就蕴含着正确的教育,但我们大部分人并不爱自己的孩子;我们希望他们成功——这意味着我们希望自己成功。不幸的是,我们是如此忙于应对头脑的各种活动,以至于我们没什么时间去提升心灵。毕竟,纪律就意味着抗拒,而抗拒能够带来爱吗?纪律只会在我们周围筑起围墙,它总是排外的,永远在制造着冲突。纪律无助于了解,因为了解是伴随着观察、伴随着摒弃一切偏见的探寻而来的。

Sensitivity can never be awakened through compulsion. One may compel a child to be outwardly quiet, but one has not come face to face with that which is making him obstinate, impudent, and so on. Compulsion breeds antagonism and fear. Reward and punishment in any form only make the mind subservient and dull; and if this is what we desire, then education through compulsion is an excellent way to proceed.

But such education cannot help us to understand the child, nor can it build a right social environment in which separatism and hatred will cease to exist. In the love of the child, right education is implied. But most of us do not love our children; we are ambitious for them — which means that we are ambitious for ourselves. Unfortunately, we are so busy with the occupations of the mind that we have little time for the promptings of the heart. After all, discipline implies resistance; and will resistance ever bring love? Discipline can only build walls about us; it is always exclusive, ever making for conflict. Discipline is not conducive to understanding; for understanding comes with observation, with inquiry in which all prejudice is set aside.

纪律是控制孩子的简便途径，但它并不能帮助孩子了解生活中所包含的各种问题。对于一大群挤在同一间教室里的学生而言，某种形式的强制和一套奖惩制度，对于维持秩序和表面上的安静来说或许是必需的；但是对于正确的教育者和为数不多的学生来说，任何压抑约束——它被委婉地称为纪律——难道是必需的吗？如果这个班级人数很少，老师就可以充分注意到每一个小孩，去观察并且帮助他，那时任何形式的强制或控制，很显然都是多余的。如果在这样一个团体中，某个学生总是不安分或者无缘无故地淘气、调皮，那么教育者就必须去研究他行为不端的原因——可能是因为饮食不当、缺少休息、家庭的纠纷或者一些潜藏的恐惧。

正确的教育中蕴含着对自由与智慧的培养，然而如果有了任何形式的强制以及强制所带来的恐惧，这件事就不可能实现了。总之，教育者需要关心的，是去帮助学生了解他整个存在的错综复杂之处。要求学生压抑他本性中的某一部分从而帮助提升其他部分，这会在他的内心造成无尽的冲突，这种冲突导致了社会的对立。只有智慧才能带来秩序，而不是纪律。

Discipline is an easy way to control a child, but it does not help him to understand the problems involved in living. Some form of compulsion, the discipline of punishment and reward, may be necessary to maintain order and seeming quietness among a large number of students herded together in a classroom; but with the right kind of educator and a small number of students, would any repression, politely called discipline, be required? If the classes are small and the teacher can give his full attention to each child, observing and helping him, then compulsion or domination in any form is obviously unnecessary. If, in such a group, a student persists in disorderliness or is unreasonably mischievous, the educator must inquire into the cause of his misbehaviour, which may be wrong diet, lack of rest, family wrangles, or some hidden fear.

Implicit in right education is the cultivation of freedom and intelligence, which is not possible if there is any form of compulsion, with its fears. After all, the concern of the educator is to help the student to understand the complexities of his whole being. To require him to suppress one part of his nature for the benefit of some other part is to create in him an endless conflict which results in social antagonisms. It is intelligence that brings order, not discipline.

正确的教育中没有遵守与顺从的立足之地。如果老师和学生没有彼此间的爱与尊重，他们之间就不可能会有合作。当孩子被要求表现出对长辈的尊敬时，这种尊敬通常会变成一个习惯，一种外在的展示，是一种将恐惧呈现为尊敬的形式。没有彼此间的尊敬和关心，就不可能有充满活力的关系——特别当老师仅仅是一个传授知识的工具时。

如果老师要求学生尊敬他，但一点儿也不尊重学生，这很显然就会导致学生这一方的冷漠和不敬。没有对人类生命的尊重，知识就只会导致毁灭和不幸。培养对他人的尊重是正确的教育必不可少的一部分，但如果教育者自身缺乏这种品质，他就无法帮助他的学生拥有完整的生活。

智慧就是洞察本质，而要洞悉本质，我们就必须摆脱头脑在寻求自身安全感和安慰的过程中所投射出来的种种障碍。只要心灵还在寻找安全感，就不可避免地会有恐惧；当人以任何方式受到严格管制时，敏锐的觉察和智慧就会遭到破坏。

Conformity and obedience have no place in the right kind of education. Cooperation between teacher and student is impossible if there is no mutual affection, mutual respect. When the showing of respect to elders is required of children, it generally becomes a habit, a mere outward performance, and fear assumes the form of veneration. Without respect and consideration, no vital relationship is possible, especially when the teacher is merely an instrument of his knowledge.

If the teacher demands respect from his pupils and has very little for them, it will obviously cause indifference and disrespect on their part. Without respect for human life, knowledge only leads to destruction and misery. The cultivation of respect for others is an essential part of right education, but if the educator himself has not this quality, he cannot help his students to an integrated life.

Intelligence is discernment of the essential, and to discern the essential there must be freedom from those hindrances which the mind projects in the search for its own security and comfort. Fear is inevitable as long as the mind is seeking security; and when human beings are regimented in any way, keen awareness and intelligence are destroyed.

教育的目的是培育正确的关系——不仅是个体之间的关系，也包括个体与社会的关系；而这就是教育首先必须帮助个体去了解他自身心理过程的原因。智慧在于了解自己，然后突破和超越自己，但只要还存在恐惧，便不会有智慧。恐惧阻碍了智慧，它是产生自我中心行为的原因之一。纪律也许能压制恐惧，却无法根除它，而我们在现代教育中所获得的肤浅知识，只是把恐惧掩藏得更深了。

当我们年轻时，无论在家中还是在学校里，我们大多数人心中都被灌输了恐惧。而父母和老师都没有耐心、时间或智慧来驱散这种幼年时期的本能恐惧。于是，当我们长大后，这种恐惧就左右了我们的态度和判断，制造出了无数的问题。正确的教育必须深入考虑恐惧的问题，因为恐惧扭曲了我们的整个人生观。脱离恐惧就是智慧的开始，而只有正确的教育才能带来摆脱恐惧的自由——唯有在这种自由中，才会有深刻的、创造性的智慧。

The purpose of education is to cultivate right relationship, between individuals, but also between the individual and society; and that is why it is essential that education should, above all, help the individual to understand his own psychological process. Intelligence lies in understanding oneself and going above and beyond oneself; but there cannot be intelligence as long as there is fear. Fear perverts intelligence and is one of the causes of self-centred action. Discipline may suppress fear but does not eradicate it, and the superficial knowledge which we receive in modern education only further conceals it.

When we are young, fear is instilled into most of us both at at school. Neither parents nor teachers have the patience, the time or the wisdom to dispel the instinctive fears of childhood, which, as we grow up, dominate our attitudes and judgment and create a great many problems. The right kind of education must take into consideration this question of fear, because fear warps our whole outlook on life. To be without fear is the beginning of wisdom, and only the right kind of education can bring about the freedom from fear in which alone there is deep and creative intelligence.

对任何行为的奖励或惩罚都只是加强了自我中心。为他人谋求利益的行动——如果它是以国家或上帝的名义——就会带来恐惧，而恐惧并不是正确行动的基础。如果我们想帮助孩子，让他变得体谅他人，我们就不该拿爱作为诱饵，而应该花时间耐心地向他解释体谅他人的方式。

当尊重别人是为了一个回报，就没有什么尊重可言了，因为那个诱饵或惩罚已经变得远比尊重之情更加重要。如果我们不尊重孩子，而只是给他一个奖赏，或者用惩罚来威胁他，那么我们就是在鼓励贪婪和恐惧。由于我们自己从小到大所受的教育，都是为了结果而行动，所以我们无法理解还有一种不为获取欲望的行动。

正确的教育将会鼓励对他人的体贴与关心，但其中没有任何的引诱或威胁。如果我们不再寻求立竿见影的结果，我们就会开始看到这一点是多么重要——那就是教育者和孩子都应该摆脱对惩罚的恐惧和对奖赏的期望，以及任何其他形式的强制。然而只要权威仍旧在关系中占有一席之地，强制就会继续存在。

Reward or punishment for any action merely strengthens self-centredness. Action for the sake of another, in the name of the country or of God, leads to fear, and fear cannot be the basis for right action. If we would help a child to be considerate of others, we should not use love as a bribe, but take the time and have the patience to explain the ways of consideration.

There is no respect for another when there is a reward for it, for the bribe or the punishment becomes far more significant than the feeling of respect. If we have no respect for the child but merely offer him a reward or threaten him with punishment, we are encouraging acquisitiveness and fear. Because we ourselves have been brought up to act for the sake of a result, we do not see that there can be action free of the desire to gain.

The right kind of education will encourage thoughtfulness and consideration for others without enticements or threats of any kind. If we no longer seek immediate results, we shall begin to see how important it is that both the educator and the child should be free from the fear of punishment and the hope of reward, and from every other form of compulsion; but compulsion will continue as long as authority is part of relationship.

如果我们从个人动机和获取利益的角度考虑，那么跟从权威会有很多好处；但是基于个人发展和利益的教育，只能建立起一种竞争不断、敌对和冷酷无情的社会结构。而我们从小就是在这种社会中被培养长大的，因此我们身上的敌意和混乱也是显而易见的。

我们一直被教导着去遵从老师或书本的权威，因为这样做有利可图。生活中每个领域里的专家们——从牧师到官僚——都在行使着权威，在支配着我们；但任何使用强制手段的政府或老师，都永远无法带来关系中的协作，而这种协作对于社会幸福来说是不可或缺的。

如果我们想让人与人之间有正确的关系，就不应该有任何强制，甚至是劝说。掌权者和屈从于权力的人之间又怎么可能会有关爱和真正的协作呢？通过冷静地思考权威的问题和它的诸多含义，通过看到对权力的渴望本身就是具有毁灭性的，就会带来一种对权威的整个运作过程的自发性的了解。一旦摒弃了权威，我们就会建立起合作关系，只有那时才会有彼此间的协作和爱。

To follow authority has many advantages if one thinks in terms of personal motive and gain; but education based on individual advancement and profit can only build a social structure which is competitive, antagonistic and ruthless. This is the kind of society in which we have been brought up, and our animosity and confusion are obvious.

We have been taught to conform to the authority of a teacher, of a book, because it is profitable to do so. The specialists in every department of life, from the priest to the bureaucrat, wield authority and dominate us; but any government or teacher that uses compulsion can never bring about the cooperation in relationship which is essential for the welfare of society.

If we are to have right relationship between human beings, there should be no compulsion nor even persuasion. How can there be affection and genuine cooperation between those who are in power and those who are subject to power? By dispassionately considering this question of authority and its many implications, by seeing that the very desire for power is in itself destructive, there comes a spontaneous understanding of the whole process of authority. The moment we discard authority we are in partnership, and only then is there cooperation and affection.

教育中真正的问题在于教育者。如果教育者把权威当成一种自我发泄的手段，如果教书对他来说是为了实现自我扩张，那么即使是一小群学生也会成为彰显他个人重要性的工具。然而，仅仅只是智力上或口头上赞同权威所带来的有害后果，也是愚蠢和无用的。

我们必须深刻洞察权威和支配背后所隐藏的种种动机。如果我们明白智慧永远无法经由强制来唤醒，那么对这个事实的觉察本身就会将我们的恐惧燃烧殆尽。然后我们就会开始培育出一个全新的环境——它将会与现有的社会秩序截然相反，并且远远超越其上。

要了解生活的意义及其冲突和痛苦，我们就必须抛开任何权威去独立思考；但如果我们出于想要帮助孩子的渴望，在他面前树立起权威的榜样，那么我们就只是鼓励了恐惧、模仿和各种形式的迷信。

The real problem in education is the educator. Even a small students becomes the instrument of his personal importance if he uses authority as a means of his own release, if teaching is for him a self-expansive fulfilment. But mere intellectual or verbal agreement concerning the crippling effects of authority is stupid and vain.

There must be deep insight into the hidden motivations of authority and domination. If we see that intelligence can never be awakened through compulsion, the very awareness of that fact will burn away our fears, and then we shall begin to cultivate a new environment which will be contrary to and far transcend the present social order.

To understand the significance of life with its conflicts and pain, we must think independently of any authority; but if in our desire to help the child we set before him authoritative examples, we shall only be encouraging fear, imitation and various forms of superstition.

具有宗教倾向的人会试图把他们的信仰、希望和恐惧强加在孩子身上——而反过来，这些东西也是他们从自己父母那里得来的；同时那些反宗教人士也同样热衷于影响孩子，使其接受自己碰巧所遵循的特定思维方式。我们都想要自己的孩子接受我们的崇拜方式，或者把我们所选择的意识形态铭记于心。陷入各种意象和公式之中是如此容易——不管这些意象和公式是我们自己发明的还是别人发明的，所以我们需要对此永远保持警觉和留心。

我们的所谓宗教，只不过是组织化的信仰及各种教条、仪式和神话。每一个宗教都有它自己的圣书、它的中间人、它的传教士，以及它控制人们的方法。我们大多数人一直都被这些东西制约着——这被认为是宗教教育；然而这种制约往往让人类彼此对立，它制造了敌意，不仅是同一宗教信徒间的敌意，也包括对其他宗教信徒的敌意。虽然所有的宗教都声称他们崇拜上帝，并且宣称人类必须相亲相爱，但他们通过奖惩的信条，把恐惧灌输给了我们，经由充满竞争性的教条，他们使猜疑和对立得以长存。

Those who are religiously inclined try to impose upon the child the beliefs, hopes and fears which they in turn have acquired from their parents; and those who are anti-religious are equally keen to influence the child to accept the particular way of thinking which they happen to follow. We all want our children to accept our form of worship or take to heart our chosen ideology. It is so easy to get entangled in images and formulations, whether invented by ourselves or by others, and therefore it is necessary to be ever watchful and alert.

What we call religion is merely organized belief, with its dogmas, rituals, and mysteries. Each religion has its own sacred book, its mediator, its priests and its ways of holding people. Most of us have been conditioned to all this, which is considered religious education; but this conditioning sets man against man, it creates antagonism, not only among the believers, but also against those of other beliefs. Though all religions assert that they worship God and say that we must love one another, they instill fear through their doctrines of reward and punishment, and through their competitive dogmas they perpetuate suspicion and antagonism.

教条、神话和仪式无益于灵性生活。真正意义上的宗教教育，乃是鼓励孩子去了解他自己与他人、与事物、与自然的关系。生活不可能脱离关系而存在，而没有自知，所有的关系——不管是和一个人的关系还是和多个人的关系——都会带来冲突和悲伤。当然了，要把这些充分地解释给一个孩子听是不可能的；但如果教育者和父母深刻领会了关系的全部意义，那么通过他们的态度、言行、举止，他们就必然可以把灵性生活的意义传达给孩子，而无须太多的言语和解释。

我们的所谓"宗教训练"没有鼓励提问和怀疑，然而，只有当我们去探寻社会和宗教加诸我们的各种价值的意义时，我们才会开始发现真实的事物。教育者的职责就是去深入检视他自己的思想和感受，丢弃那些给予他安全感和安慰的价值，因为只有那样，他才能帮助他的学生去自我觉察，去了解他们自己的各种冲动与恐惧。

Dogmas, mysteries and rituals are not conducive to a spiritual life. Religious education in the true sense is to encourage the child to understand his own relationship to people, to things and to nature. There is no existence without relationship; and without self-knowledge, all relationship, with the one and with the many, brings conflict and sorrow. Of course, to explain this fully to a child is impossible; but if the educator and the parents deeply grasp the full significance of relationship, then by their attitude, conduct and speech they will surely be able to convey to the child, without too many words and explanations, the meaning of a spiritual life.

Our so-called religious training discourages questioning and doubt, yet it is only when we inquire into the significance of the values which society and religion have placed about us that we begin to find out what is true. It is the function of the educator to examine deeply his own thoughts and feelings and to put aside those values which have given him security and comfort, for only then can he help his students to be self-aware and to understand their own urges and fears.

一个人年轻时,正是迈向正直和清明的时候,而我们这些年长者——如果我们有所了悟——就可以去帮助年轻人,让他们摆脱社会强加于他们的各种障碍,以及他们自己投射出来的障碍。如果孩子的头脑和心灵没有被宗教的先入之见和偏见塑造定型,那么他就可以经由自我了解,去自由地发现那个超越和凌驾于他自身的事物了。

真正的宗教并不是一套信仰和仪式、一些希望和恐惧;如果我们能让孩子免受这些阻碍他的影响而成长,那么或许当他成年以后,他就会开始探究真实或上帝的本质。所以,在教育孩子的过程中,深刻的洞察与了解是必需的。

大多数有宗教倾向的人,那些谈论上帝和不朽的人,并没有从根本上相信个体的自由与完整;然而,宗教就是在寻找真理的过程中去培育自由。自由是不存在妥协的。个体的局部自由根本就不是自由。任何一种制约——不管是政治上的还是宗教上的——都不是自由,也永远无法带来和平。

The time to grow straight and clear is when one is young; and those of us who are older can, if we have understanding, help the young to free themselves from the hindrances which society has imposed upon them, as well as from those which they themselves are projecting. If the child's mind and heart are not moulded by religious preconceptions and prejudices, then he will be free to discover through self-knowledge what is above and beyond himself.

True religion is not a set of beliefs and rituals, hopes and fears; and if we can allow the child to grow up without these hindering influences, then perhaps, as he matures, he will begin to inquire into the nature of reality, of God. That is why, in educating a child, deep insight and understanding are necessary.

Most people who are religiously inclined, who talk about God and immortality, do not fundamentally believe in individual freedom and integration; yet religion is the cultivation of freedom in the search for truth. There can be no compromise with freedom. Partial freedom for the individual is no freedom at all. Conditioning of any kind, whether political or religious, is not freedom and it will never bring peace.

宗教不是一种制约的形式。它是一种平和宁静的状态——其中就有真实与上帝；然而只有当具备自知和自由时，这种创造性的状态才会出现。自由会带来美德，而没有美德就不会有宁静。宁静的心灵并不是一颗受制约的心灵，它不是通过控制或训练才变得宁静的。只有当心灵了解了它自身的运作方式——也就是自我的运作方式时——宁静才会降临。

组织化的宗教就是人类僵化的思想，人类通过它建造了寺庙和教堂，它变成了胆怯者的慰藉和悲伤者的精神鸦片，但上帝或真理是远远超越思想、超越情感需求的。父母和老师，在看清了形成恐惧和悲伤的心理过程后，应当能够帮助年轻人去观察和了解他们自己的冲突和麻烦。

在孩子成长的过程中，如果我们这些大人可以帮助他们去清晰、冷静地思考，帮助他们去爱，而不是滋生仇恨，那么我们就无须再做更多了；但如果我们彼此争吵不休，如果我们无法通过深刻地转变自己从而给这个世界带来秩序与和平，那么各种宗教的圣书和神话又有什么用呢？

Religion is not a form of conditioning. It is a state of tranquillity in which there is reality, God; but that creative state can come into being only when there is self-knowledge and freedom. Freedom brings virtue, and without virtue there can be no tranquillity. The still mind is not a conditioned mind, it is not disciplined or trained to be still. Stillness comes only when the mind understands its own ways, which are the ways of the self.

Organized religion is the frozen thought of man, out of which he builds temples and churches; it has become a solace for the fearful, an opiate for those who are in sorrow. But God or truth is far beyond thought and emotional demands. Parents and teachers who recognize the psychological processes which build up fear and sorrow should be able to help the young to observe and understand their own conflicts and trials.

If we who are older can help the children, as they grow up, to think clearly and dispassionately, to love and not to breed animosity, what more is there to do? But if we are constantly at one another's throats, if we are incapable of bringing about order and peace in the world by deeply changing ourselves, of what value are the sacred books and the myths of the various religions?

真正的宗教教育，是帮助孩子去智慧地觉察，让他自己去辨别短暂和真实的事物，不偏不倚地去看待生活。在家里或者在学校里，如果能以一段认真严肃的思考或者阅读一段富有深度和意义的文字来开始我们每一天的生活，这难道不是比咕哝着一些老生常谈的话语来得更有意义吗？

过去世世代代的人，经由他们的野心、传统和理想，已经给这个世界带来了不幸与毁灭；而通过正确的教育，我们的下一代或许就可以制止这种混乱，然后建立一种更为和谐幸福的社会秩序。如果年轻人具有探究精神，如果他们在不断地寻找一切事物的真相——不管是政治的、宗教的、个人的还是周围环境的真相，那么这些年轻人就会具有重大的意义，而我们也能借此期望一个更美好的世界。

大多数孩子都抱有一颗好奇心，他们想要了解清楚一切，但他们热切的询问在我们傲慢自负的断言、我们那高高在上的不耐烦，以及我们对他们好奇心的随意漠视下而变得黯淡无光了。我们没有鼓励他们去探寻，因为我们很担心他们会问怎样的问题；我们没有培养他们的不满之情，因为我们自己已经停止了怀疑。

True religious education is to help the child to be intelligently aware, to discern for himself the temporary and the real, and to have a disinterested approach to life; and would it not have more meaning to begin each day at home or at school with a serious thought, or with a reading that has depth and significance, rather than mumble some oft-repeated words or phrases?

Past generations, with their ambitions, traditions and ideals, have brought misery and destruction to the world; perhaps the coming generations, with the right kind of education, can put an end to this chaos and build a happier social order. If those who are young have the spirit of inquiry, if they are constantly searching out the truth of all things, political and religious, personal and environmental, then youth will have great significance and there is hope for a better world.

Most children are curious, they want to know; but their eager inquiry is dulled by our pontifical assertions, our superior impatience and our casual brushing aside of their curiosity. We do not encourage their inquiry, for we are rather apprehensive of what may be asked of us; we do not foster their discontent, for we ourselves have ceased to question.

大多数父母和老师都害怕不满之情,因为它打扰了各种形式的安全感,因此他们鼓励年轻人借着安稳的工作、继承遗产、婚姻以及宗教教义的安慰来压制这种不满。年纪大的人熟知各种使头脑和心灵变得迟钝的方法,于是他们通过使年轻人铭记各种权威、传统和信仰——这些他们自己已经接受的东西——来继续让孩子变得和他们一样麻木、迟钝。

只有通过鼓励孩子去质疑书本——无论是什么书——去探究现有社会价值、传统、政体和宗教信仰等等的正确性时,教育者和父母才有希望唤醒并保持孩子批判性的警觉和敏锐的洞察。

年轻人——如果他们真的是有生气的年轻人——都是充满希望和不满之情的,这是必然的,否则他们就已经衰老和死亡了。而年长的人,他们曾经不满过,但如今已经成功地闷熄了不满的火焰,并且通过各种途径找到了安全感和舒适感。他们渴望自己和自己的家庭能永远延续下去,他们热切地渴望观念、关系和占有物带来的确定感;所以每当他们感到不满时,他们便会全神贯注地投入到他们的各种责任、工作或任何其他事情中去,以此来逃避那种令人烦扰的不满情绪。

Most parents and teachers are afraid of discontent because it is disturbing to all forms of security, and so they encourage the young to overcome it through safe jobs, inheritance, marriage and the consolation of religious dogmas. Elders, knowing only too well the many ways of blunting the mind and the heart, proceed to make the child as dull as they are by impressing upon him the authorities, traditions and beliefs which they themselves have accepted.

Only by encouraging the child to question the book, whatever it be, to inquire into the validity of the existing social values, traditions, forms of government, religious beliefs and so on, can the educator and the parents hope to awaken and sustain his critical alertness and keen insight.

The young, if they are at all alive, are full of hope and discontent; they must be, otherwise they are already old and dead. And the old are those who were once discontented, but who have successfully smothered that flame and have found security and comfort in various ways. They crave permanency for themselves and their families, they ardently desire certainty in ideas, in relationships, in possessions; so the moment they feel discontented, they become absorbed in their responsibilities, in their jobs, or in anything else, in order to escape from that disturbing feeling of discontent.

当我们年轻时，应该心怀不满，不仅对自己不满，也对我们周围的事物不满。我们应该学会清晰地思考而不带任何偏见，由此内心便不会有依赖与恐惧。独立并不是指地图上那一块涂抹了颜色的区域——我们把它称为祖国——独立是针对我们个体而言的；虽然外在我们是彼此依赖的，但如果我们内在已经摆脱了对权力、地位和权威的渴望，那么外在的相互依赖就不会变得残酷或带有压迫性。

我们必须了解不满——这个我们大多数人都害怕的东西。不满或许会带来好像是混乱的东西，但如果它通往的是——它本应如此——自我了解和自我舍弃的话，它就会创造出一种崭新的社会秩序与持久的和平。伴随着自我舍弃，无限的喜悦就会降临。

不满是通向自由的途径，但要不带偏见地探寻，我们就一定不能有任何感情上的损耗，这种感情的损耗常常表现为政治集会的形式，表现为高呼口号、寻找古鲁或灵性导师，以及各种宗教名义下的纵欲。这些消耗让头脑和心灵变得迟钝，使它们无力去洞察，由此便很容易被环境和恐惧塑造。只有强烈的探寻欲望——而不是简单地去模仿众人——才能带来对于生活方式的全新理解。

While we are young is the time to be discontented, not only with ourselves, but also with the things about us. We should learn clearly and without bias, so as not to be inwardly dependent and Independence is not for that coloured section of the map which our country, but for ourselves as individuals; and though outwardly we are dependent on one another, this mutual dependence does not become cruel or oppressive if inwardly we are free of the craving for power, position and authority.

We must understand discontent, of which most of us are afraid. Discontent may bring what appears to be disorder; but if it leads, as it should, to self- knowledge and self-abnegation, then it will create a new social order and enduring peace. With self-abnegation comes immeasurable joy.

Discontent is the means to freedom; but in order to inquire without bias, there must be none of the emotional dissipation which often takes the form of political gatherings, the shouting of slogans, the search for a guru or spiritual teacher, and religious orgies of different kinds. This dissipation dulls the mind and heart, making them incapable of insight and therefore easily moulded by circumstances and fear. It is the burning desire to inquire, and not the easy imitation of the multitude, that will bring about a new understanding of the ways of life.

年轻人是如此容易被牧师、政客、富人或穷人说服，而去依照特定的方式思考；但正确的教育应当帮助他们注意到这些影响，这样他们就不会鹦鹉学舌般地去重复口号或者掉入任何贪婪——不管是他们自己的贪婪还是别人的贪婪的狡猾陷阱中。他们绝不能允许权威扼杀他们的头脑和心灵。跟随他人——不管那人多么伟大，或者墨守于令人满足的意识形态，都无法带来一个和平的世界。

当我们离开学校或大学后，很多人就扔掉了书本，好像觉得我们的学习就到此为止了；还有一些人被激励着去思考更深远的领域，他们不停地看书，吸收别人所说的东西，沉溺于知识中。只要还存在对知识或技术的崇拜，把它作为一种通向成功和支配的途径，就必然会有无情的竞争、对立和为了谋生的无尽奋斗。

只要我们的目标还是成功，我们便无法摆脱恐惧，因为对成功的渴望不可避免地带来了对失败的恐惧。这就是为什么我们不应该教导年轻人去崇拜成功的原因。大多数人都在寻求某种形式的成功——不管是在网球场上、生意场上，还是在政治领域。我们都想要爬到顶端，这种欲望制造出了我们内心以及我们和邻居之间的持续不断的冲突；它导致了竞争、妒忌和仇恨，最终引发了战争。

The young are so easily persuaded by the priest or the politician, by the rich or the poor, to think in a particular way; but the right kind of education should help them to be watchful of these influences so that they do not repeat slogans like parrots or fall into any cunning trap of greed, whether their own or that of another. They must not allow authority to stifle their minds and hearts. To follow another, however great, or to give one's adherence to a gratifying ideology, will not bring about a peaceful world.

When we leave school or college, many of us put away books and seem to feel that we are done with learning; and there are those who are stimulated to think further afield, who keep on reading and absorbing what others have said, and become addicted to knowledge. As long as there is the worship of knowledge or technique as a means to success and dominance, there must be ruthless competition, antagonism and the ceaseless struggle for bread.

As long as success is our goal we cannot be rid of fear, for the desire to succeed inevitably breeds the fear of failure. That is why the young should not be taught to worship success. Most people seek success in one form or another, whether on the tennis court, in the business world, or in politics. We all want to be on top, and this desire creates constant conflict within ourselves and with our neighbours; it leads to competition, envy, animosity and finally to war.

就像老一辈人一样，年轻人同样也在寻求成功和安全，虽然起初他们或许有些不满之情，但很快他们也变成了受人尊敬的体面人，于是便害怕再对社会说"不"了。他们自己的欲望之墙开始封闭他们，他们开始担当起了权威的角色。而他们的不满——也就是探究、寻找和了解的火焰——变得暗淡，然后逐渐消失了，取而代之的是想要一份更好的工作、找个有钱人结婚或者事业成功，而这一切都是在渴望更多的安全感。

年老之人和年轻人并没有什么本质区别，两者都是他们自身欲望与满足的奴隶。成熟与年龄无关，它是伴随着了解而到来的。强烈的探寻精神对年轻人来说或许更容易一些，因为年老之人已经饱受生活的蹂躏，各种冲突已经把他们折磨得筋疲力尽，而死亡正以不同的方式在等待着他们。不过，这并不意味着他们无法进行有目的的探寻，只不过对他们来说比较困难罢了。

Like the older generation, the young also seek success and security; though at first they may be discontented, they soon become respectable and are afraid to say no to society. The walls of their own desires begin to enclose them, and they assume the reins of authority. Their discontent, which is the very flame of inquiry, of search, of understanding, grows dull and dies away, and in its place there comes the desire for a better job, a rich marriage, a successful career, all of which is the craving for more security.

There is no essential difference between the old and the young, for both are slaves to their own desires and gratifications. Maturity is not a matter of age, it comes with understanding. The ardent spirit of inquiry is perhaps easier for the young, because those who are older have been battered about by life, conflicts have worn them out and death in different forms awaits them. This does not mean that they are incapable of purposive inquiry, but only that it is more difficult for them.

很多成年人并不成熟，而且相当幼稚，这就是助长了这个世界的混乱和不幸的原因。年长者要对如今普遍的经济和道德危机负责，而我们最不幸的弱点之一，就是想要别人来替我们行动，然后改变我们生活的进程。我们坐等其他人起来反抗，然后去重建一切，而我们自己依然毫无行动——直到我们确信能有一个结果为止。

我们大多数人所追求的是安全和成功；但一颗寻找安全、渴望成功的心灵并不是智慧的心灵，因此它无法去完整地行动。只有当一个人觉察到他自身的局限，觉察到自己种族、国家、政治和宗教的偏见——也就是意识到自我的各种运作方式永远是分离性的——那时才会有完整的行动。

生命是一泓深泉。你可以带着一个小桶来到它跟前，只取一点点水；或者可以带一个大桶过去，汲取大量滋润和供养你的泉水。一个人年轻时，就是去探究和尝试每一样事物的时候。学校应当帮助年轻人找到他们的天职和责任，而不仅仅是把事实数据和技术知识塞满他们的头脑；它应该成为一片沃土，让年轻人可以在其中无惧、快乐、完整地成长。

Many adults are immature and rather childish, and this is a contributing cause of the confusion and misery in the world. It is the older people who are responsible for the prevailing economic and moral crisis; and one of our unfortunate weaknesses is that we want someone else to act for us and change the course of our lives. We wait for others to revolt and build anew, and we remain inactive until we are assured of the outcome.

It is security and success that most of us are after; and a mind that is seeking security, that craves success, is not intelligent, and is therefore incapable of integrated action. There can be integrated action only if one is aware of one's own conditioning, of one's racial, national, political and religious prejudices; that is, only if one realizes that the ways of the self are ever separative.

Life is a well of deep waters. One can come to it with small buckets and draw only a little water, or one can come with large vessels, drawing plentiful waters that will nourish and sustain. While one is young is the time to investigate, to experiment with everything. The school should help its young people to discover their vocations and responsibilities, and not merely cram their minds with facts and technical knowledge; it should be the soil in which they can grow without fear, happily and integrally.

教育孩子就是帮助他理解自由和完整。要自由就必须有秩序，而唯有美德才能带来秩序；只有当有了极度的简单时，完整才会产生。我们必须从无尽的复杂慢慢转变为简单；我们内在的生命和外在的需求都必须变得简单。

当今的教育关心的是外在的效率，它忽视或故意曲解了人类的内在本性，它只发展了人身上的某一部分，而让其他部分自生自灭。然而我们内在的混乱、敌对和恐惧总是会胜过外在的社会结构——不管这个结构被构想得多么高尚，或是被建造得多么精巧。没有正确的教育，我们就会互相毁灭，于是每个人外在的安全便会失去。正确地教育学生就是帮助他了解他自己整体的运作过程，因为只有当日常行为中有了头脑与心灵的融合，才会有智慧和内在的转变。

To educate a child is to help him to understand freedom and integration. To have freedom there must be order, which virtue alone can give; and integration can take place only when there is great simplicity. From innumerable complexities we must grow to simplicity; we must become simple in our inward life and in our outward needs.

Education is at present concerned with outward efficiency, and it disregards, or deliberately perverts, the inward nature of man; it only one part of him and leaves the rest to drag along as best it inner confusion, antagonism and fear ever overcome the outer society, however nobly conceived and cunningly built. When the right kind of education we destroy one another, and physical security for every individual is denied. To educate the student rightly is to help him to understand the total process of himself; for it is only when there is integration of the mind and heart in everyday action that there can be intelligence and inward transformation.

在提供信息和技术培训的同时，教育首先应该鼓励一种整体的生活观，它应当帮助学生认清和打破他内心所有社会等级的差别和偏见，并且不鼓励对于权力和支配的贪婪追求。它应该鼓励正确的自我观察，鼓励学生去经历完整的生活——不去赋予某个部分、赋予"我"和"我的"以重要的意义，而是帮助心灵凌驾和超越自身，从而发现那个真实。

只有通过我们日常活动中的自我了解——日常活动就是我们和他人、事物、观念以及自然的关系——自由才会降临。如果教育者是在帮助学生变得完整，他就不会狂热或过度地强调生活中的任何一个方面。正是对生活整体过程的了解带来了完整。当有了自我了解，制造错觉的力量就会止息，只有那时才可能会有真实或上帝。

While offering information and technical training, education should above all encourage an integrated outlook on life; it should help the student to recognize and break down in himself all social distinctions and prejudices, and discourage the acquisitive pursuit of power and domination. It should encourage the right kind of self-observation and the experiencing of life as a whole, which is not to give significance to the part, to the "me" and the "mine", but to help the mind to go above and beyond itself to discover the real.

Freedom comes into being only through self-knowledge in one's daily occupations, that is, in one's relationship with people, with things, with ideas and with nature. If the educator is helping the student to be integrated, there can be no fanatical or unreasonable emphasis on any particular phase of life. It is the understanding of the total process of existence that brings integration. When there is self-knowledge, the power of creating illusions ceases, and only then is it possible for reality or God to be.

如果人类想在不让自己粉身碎骨的情况下摆脱掉任何危机——尤其是当今世界的危机，他们就必须保持完整；所以对于那些真正对教育感兴趣的父母和老师而言，最主要的问题就是如何培养出一个完整的人。要实现这一点，教育者自己很显然必须是完整的；所以正确的教育极其重要，不仅是对于年轻人而言，同样也包括老一辈的人——如果他们愿意去学习，并且还没有变得太固执的话。我们内心是什么样子的，远比"我们要教给孩子什么"这个老问题更重要，如果我们爱自己的孩子，就会努力使他们拥有正确的教育者。

教书不应该成为一种专家的职业。当它成为职业——通常都会如此——爱就会逐渐消退；而爱是达到完整的过程中所必需的。要完整，就必须摆脱恐惧。无所畏惧带来了独立性——这种独立性中没有冷酷无情，也没有对他人的蔑视——而独立性是生命中最不可或缺的因素。没有爱，我们无法解决无数矛盾冲突的问题；没有爱，获取知识只会增加混乱并且导致自我毁灭。

Human beings must be integrated if they are to come out of and especially the present world crisis, without being broken; therefore, to parents and teachers who are really interested in education, the main problem is how to develop an integrated individual. To do this, the educator himself must obviously be integrated; so the right kind of education is of the highest importance, not only for the young, but also for the older generation if they are willing to learn and are not too set in their ways. What we are in ourselves is much more important than the traditional question of what to teach the child, and if we love our children we will see to it that they have the right kind of educators.

Teaching should not become a specialist's profession. When it does, as is so often the case, love fades away; and love is essential to the process of integration. To be integrated there must be freedom from fear. Fearlessness brings independence without ruthlessness, without contempt for another, and this is the most essential factor in life. Without love we cannot work out our many conflicting problems; without love the acquisition of knowledge only increases confusion and leads to self-destruction.

一个完整的人将会通过体验来获得技巧,因为创作的冲动会造就其自身的技巧——这才是最伟大的艺术。当小孩有了想画画的创作冲动,他就去画了,他不会去操心什么技巧。同样,那些对生活有所体验从而去教育孩子的人——他们才是真正的老师,而他们也将创造出他们自己的教学技巧。

这听起来很简单,但它其实是一次深刻的革命。如果我们思考一下,就会明白它将会给这个社会带来的非凡影响。如今,我们大多数人到了四十五岁或五十岁时,个个都已被每日重复的工作奴役折磨得筋疲力尽了;顺从、恐惧和容忍已经毁掉了我们,尽管我们仍在社会上——除了对统治者而言,这个社会其实并没有什么意义——努力奋斗着并且感到安全。如果老师看到了这一点,并且自身也确实有所体会,那么不管他的脾气怎样、能力如何,他的教学都不会成为一种例行公事,而是会变成帮助学生的工具。

The integrated human being will come to technique through experiencing, for the creative impulse makes its own technique — and that is the greatest art. When a child has the creative impulse to paint, he paints, he does not bother about technique. Likewise people who are experiencing, and therefore teaching, are the only real teachers, and they too will create their own technique.

This sounds very simple, but it is really a deep revolution. If we think about it we can see the extraordinary effect it will have on society. At present most of us are washed out at the age of forty-five or fifty by slavery to routine; through compliance, through fear and acceptance, we are finished, though we struggle on in a society that has very little meaning except for those who dominate it and are secure. If the teacher sees this and is himself really experiencing, then whatever his temperament and capacities may be, his teaching will not be a matter of routine but will become an instrument of help.

要了解一个孩子，我们必须观察他玩耍，研究他的各种情绪；我们不能把自己的偏见、希望和恐惧投射到他身上，也不能塑造他，让他符合我们的欲望所设定的模板。如果我们总是不断地根据自己个人的喜好来评判孩子，就必然会在我们和他的关系中，以及他与世界的关系中制造屏障与阻碍。但不幸的是，我们大多数人都希望以一种能够满足我们个人虚荣心和癖好的方式来塑造孩子；在对孩子独家的占有和支配中，我们找到了不同程度的安慰与满足。

毫无疑问，这种过程并非关系，而只是一种强迫，因此，重要的是去了解那种深奥复杂的支配欲。这种欲望以很多微妙的形式呈现；它很自以为是——这是它非常根深蒂固的一点。那种想要去"服务他人"的愿望里，就带着潜意识里想要去支配的渴望——这一点我们很难理解。当有了占有，还会有爱吗？在我们和我们设法去控制的人之间，能产生交流吗？支配就是利用他人来满足自我，如果你利用他人，就不会有爱。

To understand a child we have to watch him at play, study different moods; we cannot project upon him our own prejudices, and fears, or mould him to fit the pattern of our desires. If we are constantly judging the child according to our personal likes and dislikes, we are bound to create barriers and hindrances in our relationship with him and in his relationships with the world. Unfortunately, most of us desire to shape the child in a way that is gratifying to our own vanities and idiosyncrasies; we find varying degrees of comfort and satisfaction in exclusive ownership and domination.

Surely, this process is not relationship, but mere imposition, and it is therefore essential to understand the difficult and complex desire to dominate. It takes many subtle forms; and in its self-righteous aspect, it is very obstinate. The desire to "serve" with the unconscious longing to dominate is difficult to understand. Can there be love where there is possessiveness? Can we be in communion with those whom we seek to control? To dominate is to use another for self-gratification, and where there is the use of another there is no love.

当有了爱，便会有关心，不只是关心孩子，而是关心每一个人。除非我们被这个问题深深触动，否则我们永远无法找到正确的教育方式。仅有技术的培训必然导致冷酷无情，要教育我们的孩子，我们就必须对生活的全部运动保持敏感。我们所想的东西，我们所做的事情，我们所说的话——这一切都至关重要，因为它们会创造出一种环境，这种环境要么帮助了孩子，要么就是阻碍了他。

因此，我们当中对这个问题深感兴趣的人，很显然必须开始了解自己，从而有助于去转变这个社会；我们会把创造新的教育方法作为自己直接的责任。如果我们爱自己的孩子，我们难道不会找出一条终止战争的途径吗？但如果我们仅仅使用"爱"这个字眼，却没有什么实质内容的话，那么关于人类痛苦与不幸的整个复杂问题就仍将继续存在。这个问题的出路在于我们自身。我们必须开始了解我们与自己同伴的关系，我们与自然、观念和各种事物的关系，因为没有那份了解，便不会有希望，也就没有任何途径可以摆脱冲突和痛苦。

When there is love there is consideration, not only for the for every human being. Unless we are deeply touched by the problem, we will never find the right way of education. Mere technical training inevitably makes for ruthlessness, and to educate our children we must be sensitive to the whole movement of life. What we think, what we do, what we say matters infinitely, because it creates the environment, and the environment either helps or hinders the child.

Obviously, then, those of us who are deeply interested in this problem will have to begin to understand ourselves and thereby help to transform society; we will make it our direct responsibility to bring about a new approach to education. If we love our children, will we not find a way of putting an end to war? But if we are merely using the word "love" without substance, then the whole complex problem of human misery will remain. The way out of this problem lies through ourselves. We must begin to understand our relationship with our fellow men, with nature, with ideas and with things, for without that understanding there is no hope, there is no way out of conflict and suffering.

养育一个孩子需要智慧的观察以及关爱。专家和他们的知识永远无法取代父母的爱。然而，大多数父母由于他们自身的恐惧和野心——这些东西局限和扭曲了孩子的视野——已经腐化了那份爱。所以我们中很少有人关心爱，大多数人只是热衷于爱的表象。

如今的教育和社会结构并不能帮助个体走向自由和完整；如果父母真的很认真，并且渴望孩子可以逐渐发展出他充分完整的能力，他们就必须开始改变家庭所带来的影响，并且开始建立一些拥有正确教育者的学校。

家庭的影响和学校的影响之间绝不能有任何矛盾，因此父母和老师都必须重新教育自己。个体的私生活和他作为群体成员的生活常常是矛盾的，这种矛盾制造出了个体内心以及他的关系中无止境的战争。

这种冲突经由错误的教育受到了鼓励和支持，孩子的内心从一开始就已经被割裂了，这导致了个人和社会的灾难。

The bringing up of a child requires intelligent observation and care. Experts and their knowledge can never replace the parents' love, but most parents corrupt that love by their own fears and ambitions, which condition and distort the outlook of the child. So few of us are concerned with love, but we are vastly taken up with the appearance of love.

The present educational and social structure does not help the individual towards freedom and integration; and if the parents are at all in earnest and desire that the child shall grow to his fullest integral capacity, they must begin to alter the influence of the home and set about creating schools with the right kind of educators.

The influence of the home and that of the school must not be in any way contradictory, so both parents and teachers must re-educate themselves. The contradiction which so often exists between the private life of the individual and his life as a member of the group creates an endless battle within himself and in his relationships.

This conflict is encouraged and sustained through the wrong kind of education, The child is divided within himself from the very start, which results in personal and social disasters.

如果我们当中那些爱自己的孩子的人，那些看到了这个问题的急迫性的人，能够全身心投入去处理这个问题，那么，不管我们的人数多么少，经由正确的教育和明智的家庭氛围，我们就可以帮助培养出完整的人；然而，如果我们像多数人一样，用头脑的狡猾填满自己的心灵，那么我们就将继续看着自己的孩子被战争、饥荒和他们自己的心理冲突摧毁。

　　正确的教育伴随着我们自身的转变而来。我们必须重新教育自己，教育自己不要为任何理由——不管是多么正义的理由——而自相残杀；也不要为了任何意识形态——不管它看起来多么有希望给这个世界带来幸福的未来——而彼此杀戮。我们必须学会同情、学会知足常乐，然后去寻找那个至高之物，只有那时，人类才会获得真正的拯救。

If those of us who love our children and see the urgency of this problem will set our minds and hearts to it, then, however few we may be, through right education and an intelligent home environment, we can help to bring about integrated human beings; but if, like so many others, we fill our hearts with the cunning things of the mind, then we shall continue to see our children destroyed in wars, in famines, and by their own psychological conflicts.

Right education comes with the transformation of ourselves. We must re-educate ourselves not to kill one another for any cause, however righteous, for any ideology, however promising it may appear to be for the future happiness of the world. We must learn to be compassionate, to be content with little, and to seek the Supreme, for only then can there be the true salvation of mankind.

第三章
智力、权威和智慧

CHAPTER III

INTELLECT, AUTHORITY AND INTELLIGENCE

我们很多人似乎认为，通过教每个人读书写字，就可以解决人类的问题。这种想法已经被证明是错误的。那些所谓"受过教育"的人，并不是热爱和平的、完整的人，这些人对这个世界的混乱与不幸同样负有责任。

正确的教育意味着唤醒智慧，培养一种完整的生活，只有这种教育才能够创造出一种全新的文化以及一个和平的世界；然而，要带来这种新的教育，我们必须在一个完全不同的基础上重新开始。

眼看着这个世界在我们周围化为废墟，我们却在讨论各种理论和毫无意义的政治问题，玩弄一些浮于表面的改革。这难道不是表明我们完全没有任何思考吗？有些人或许同意这一点，但他们仍将一如既往地做着同样的事，这就是我们生活的悲哀。当我们听到了真理却没有据此行动时，真理就会变成我们内心的毒药，这种毒药会蔓延扩散，带来心理上的困扰、失衡与病态。唯有唤醒个体内心创造性的智慧，才可能会有和平与幸福的生活。

Many of us seem to think that by teaching every human being to read and write, we shall solve our human problems; but this idea has proved to be false. The so-called educated are not peace-loving, integrated people, and they too are responsible for the confusion and misery of the world.

The right kind of education means the awakening of intelligence, the fostering of an integrated life, and only such education can create a new culture and a peaceful world; but to bring about this new kind of education, we must make a fresh start on an entirely different basis.

With the world falling into ruin about us, we discuss theories political questions, and play with superficial reforms. Does this not indicate utter thoughtlessness on our part? Some may agree that it does, but they will go on doing exactly as they have always done — and that is the sadness of existence. When we hear a truth and do not act upon it, it becomes a poison within ourselves, and that poison spreads, bringing psychological disturbances, unbalance and ill health. Only when creative intelligence is awakened in the individual is there a possibility of a peaceful and happy life.

仅仅通过更替一个新政府，更替一个新政党、新阶级或者新的剥削者，我们是无法变得智慧的。流血的革命永远无法解决我们的问题。只有深刻的内在革命——它会改变我们所有的价值——才能创造出一种截然不同的环境和智慧的社会结构，而这种革命只有你我能够带来。除非我们作为个体打破了自身的心理障碍并获得了自由，否则就不会诞生出新的秩序。

我们可以在纸上描绘出灿烂的乌托邦蓝图，一个美好的新世界；然而，以牺牲现在的代价来期待一个未知的未来，这无疑永远无法解决我们的任何问题。现在与未来之间夹杂着如此多的因素，以至于没人知道未来会是什么样。如果我们非常真诚，那么我们能够做的，并且必须要做的就是立即处理我们的问题，而不是把它们拖延到未来。永恒不是在未来，永恒就是现在。我们的问题存在于此刻，唯有在此刻这些问题才能得到解决。

我们中那些认真的人必须革新自己，然而只有当我们放弃了那些价值——那些我们经由自我保护和侵略好斗的欲望而制造出来的价值——我们才会获得新生。自我了解是自由的起点，只有当我们知晓了自己，才能带来秩序与和平。

We cannot be intelligent by merely substituting one government for another, one party or class for another, one exploiter for another. Bloody revolution can never solve our problems. Only a profound inward revolution which alters all our values can create a different environment, an intelligent social structure, and such a revolution can be brought about only by you and me. No new order will arise until we individually break down our own psychological barriers and are free.

On paper we can draw the blueprints for a brilliant Utopia, a brave new world; but the sacrifice of the present to an unknown future will certainly never solve any of our problems. There are so many elements intervening between now and the future, that no man can know what the future will be. What we can and must do if we are in earnest, is to tackle our problems now, and not postpone them to the future. Eternity is not in the future; eternity is now. Our problems exist in the present, and it is only in the present that they can be solved.

Those of us who are serious must regenerate ourselves; but there can be regeneration only when we break away from those values which we have created through our self-protective and aggressive desires. Self-knowledge is the beginning of freedom, and it is only when we know ourselves that we can bring about order and peace.

然而，有些人也许会问："单单一个人又能做些什么来影响历史呢？人真的可以通过他的生活方式来改变任何东西吗？"当然可以了。你和我显然无法制止迫在眉睫的战争，或者让不同的国家立即彼此谅解；但至少我们可以在自己日常关系的范围里实现一次根本的改变，这种改变自然会产生其效果。

个体的觉悟的确会影响到一大群人，但前提是他不渴望得到结果。如果他想的是获取利益和产生影响力，正确的转变就不可能发生在他身上了。

人类的问题并不简单，它们是非常复杂的。要了解这些问题需要耐心和洞察，而最重要的是我们作为个体，要亲自去了解和解决它们。通过简单的公式或口号，我们无法了解它们；我们也无法依靠专家们特定方式的工作，在问题自身单一的层面去解决问题，这样做只会导致更大的混乱与不幸。只有当我们把自己作为一个整体过程加以觉察——也就是当我们了解了我们所有的心理构成时——无数的问题才能被我们了解和解决；然而，没有一个宗教领袖或政治领袖可以给予我们打开这种了解的钥匙。

Now, some may ask, "What can a single individual do that history? Can he accomplish anything at all by the way he lives?" Certainly he can. You and I are obviously not going to stop the immediate wars, or create an instantaneous understanding between nations; but at least we can bring about, in the world of our everyday relationships, a fundamental change which will have its own effect.

Individual enlightenment does affect large groups of people, one is not eager for results. If one thinks in terms of gain and transformation of oneself is not possible.

Human problems are not simple, they are very complex. To them requires patience and insight, and it is of the highest importance that we as individuals understand and resolve them for ourselves. They are not to be understood through easy formulas or slogans; nor can they be solved at their own level by specialists working along a particular line, which only leads to further confusion and misery. Our many problems can be understood and resolved only when we are aware of ourselves as a total process, that is, when we understand our whole psychological make-up; and no religious or political leader can give us the key to that understanding.

要了解我们自己,就必须觉察我们的关系——不仅是我们和人的关系,也包括我们和财产、观念、自然的关系。如果我们要带来一次人类关系中真正的革命——人类关系是所有社会的基础——我们自身的价值观和视野就必须彻底改变;但我们回避这种我们自身所必需的、根本的改变,而试图在这个世界上掀起一些政治革命——这些革命往往导致了流血和灾难。

建立在感觉之上的关系,永远无法成为自我解脱的手段;然而我们大部分的关系都是建立在感觉之上的,它们是我们渴望一己私利、渴望安慰和内心安全感的产物。虽然它们也许能让我们暂时脱离自我,但这种关系只会加强自我及其封闭和束缚性的活动。关系是一面镜子,从中我们可以看到自我及其所有的活动;然而只有当我们通过关系中的种种反应了解自我的运作方式,才能创造性地从自我中解脱出来。

To understand ourselves, we must be aware of our relationship, not only with people, but also with property, with ideas and with nature. If we are to bring about a true revolution in human relationship, which is the basis of all society, there must be a fundamental change in our own values and outlook; but we avoid the necessary and fundamental transformation of ourselves, and try to bring about political revolutions in the world, which always leads to bloodshed and disaster.

Relationship based on sensation can never be a means of the self; yet most of our relationships are based on sensation, they are the outcome of our desire for personal advantage, for comfort, for psychological security. Though they may offer us a momentary escape from the self, such relationships only give strength to the self, with its enclosing and binding activities. Relationship is a mirror in which the self and all its activities can be seen; and it is only when the ways of the self are understood in the reactions of relationship that there is creative release from the self.

要改变这个世界，我们内在必须有一种重生。依靠暴力和简单的彼此清算是做不成任何事情的。我们或许可以通过加入某些团体，通过研究社会和经济改革的方法，通过颁布法律或者通过祈祷来找到一种短暂的释放，但无论做什么，如果没有自我了解以及自我了解内在中所有的爱，我们的问题就会不断扩大和增加。然而，如果我们可以全身心地投入到这个了解自己的任务中去，那么毫无疑问，我们就能解决无数的冲突和悲伤了。

现代教育正在把我们变成毫无思想的存在体，它并没有做点什么来帮助我们找到个人的天职。我们通过了某些考试，然后如果运气好的话，我们会得到一份工作——这通常意味着我们将会在无止境的例行公事中度过余生。我们也许并不喜欢自己的工作，但我们不得不硬着头皮干下去，因为我们没有其他的谋生手段。我们也许想做一些完全不同的事，然而各种义务和责任压住了我们，而我们也受困于自己的忧虑和恐惧。因为遭受了挫折，于是我们就通过性、酗酒、政治或者充满幻想的宗教来寻求逃避。

To transform the world, there must be regeneration within Nothing can be achieved by violence, by the easy liquidation of one another. We may find a temporary release by joining groups, by studying methods of social and economic reform, by enacting legislation, or by praying; but do what we will, without self-knowledge and the love that is inherent in it, our problems will ever expand and multiply. Whereas, if we apply our minds and hearts to the task of knowing ourselves, we shall undoubtedly solve our many conflicts and sorrows.

Modern education is making us into thoughtless entities; it little towards helping us to find our individual vocation. We pass examinations and then, with luck, we get a job — which often endless routine for the rest of our life. We may dislike our job, but we are forced to continue with it because we have no other means of We may want to do something entirely different, but responsibilities hold us down, and we are hedged in by our own anxieties and fears. Being frustrated, we seek escape through sex, drink, politics or fanciful religion.

当我们的野心遭到挫败后，我们便会过分重视那些本应十分寻常的事物，于是我们的心理产生了扭曲。除非我们对自己的生活，对爱，对我们在政治、宗教和社会中的欲望及其需求以及它们所造成的阻碍，有了全面、广泛的了解，否则我们在关系中的问题仍将与日俱增，给我们带来不幸与毁灭。

无知是对自我的运作方式缺乏了解，这种无知无法通过浮于表面的行动和改革来加以消除。只有当我们不断地觉察自我在其所有关系中的各种活动和反应时，才能消除无知。

我们必须明白的是，我们不仅仅受限于环境，而且我们就是环境，我们并不是某种与之分离的东西。我们的思想和反应受制于社会所强加于我们的种种价值——我们就是这个社会的一部分。

When our ambitions are thwarted, we give undue importance to that which should be normal, and we develop a psychological twist. Until we have a comprehensive understanding of our life and love, of our political, religious and social desires, with their demands and hindrances, we shall have ever-increasing problems in our relationships, leading us to misery and destruction.

Ignorance is lack of knowledge of the ways of the self, and this ignorance cannot be dissipated by superficial activities and reforms; it can be dissipated only by one's constant awareness of the movements and responses of the self in all its relationships.

What we must realize is that we are not only conditioned by environment, but that we are the environment — we are not something apart from it. Our thoughts and responses are conditioned by the values which society, of which we are a part, has imposed upon us.

我们从未看到自己就是整个环境，因为我们内心有好多个存在体，这些存在体都在围绕着"我""自我"而运转着。自我就是由这些存在体组成的，而这些存在体只不过是形形色色的欲望。从这些聚集在一起的欲望中就产生出了那个中心人物——也就是思想者，那个"我"和"我的"的意志；由此在"我"与"非我"之间，在"我"与环境或社会之间就形成了一种分裂。这种割裂就是内在和外在冲突的开始。

觉察到这整个过程——既包括意识层面的，也包括潜藏深处的——就是冥想；经由这种冥想就可以超越自我及其欲望与冲突。要摆脱给予自我庇护的种种影响和价值，就需要有自我了解；唯有在这份摆脱了各种影响和价值的自由中，才会有创造、真理、上帝或者不管你称之为什么。

舆论和传统从我们很小的时候起，就开始塑造我们的思想和感觉。那些直接的影响和印象会产生一种强大而持久的效果，它造就了我们有意识生活和潜意识生活的整个过程。在我们还是小孩的时候，由于教育以及社会的影响，循规蹈矩的行为就已经开始了。

We never see that we are the total environment because there are several entities in us, all revolving around the "me", the self. The self is made up of these entities, which are merely desires in various forms. From this conglomeration of desires arises the central figure, the thinker, the will of the "me" and the "mine"; and a division is thus established between the self and the not-self, between the "me" and the environment or society. This separation is the beginning of conflict, inward and outward.

Awareness of this whole process, both the conscious and the hidden, is meditation; and through this meditation the self, with its desires and conflicts, is transcended. Self-knowledge is necessary if one is to be free of the influences and values that give shelter to the self; and in this freedom alone is there creation, truth, God, or what you will.

Opinion and tradition mould our thoughts and feelings from the tenderest age. The immediate influences and impressions produce an effect which is powerful and lasting, and which shapes the whole course of our conscious and unconscious life. Conformity begins in childhood through education and the impact of society.

渴望去模仿——不仅仅是表面的模仿，也包括内心深处的模仿——是我们生活中一个非常强有力的因素，我们几乎没有什么独立的思考和感受。即使当它们真的出现时，也只不过是一些被动的反应，因此它并没有脱离既定的模式，因为在被动反应中是没有自由可言的。

哲学和宗教已经制订了一些方法，说我们可以通过这些方法去了悟真理或上帝；然而，仅仅遵循某个方法依然是毫无思考和不完整的——不管那个方法看起来多么有益于我们日常的社会生活。想要去遵从的强烈渴望——对安全感的渴望——滋生了恐惧，并彰显了那些政治和宗教的权威、那些领袖和英雄——他们鼓励恭敬顺从，而我们则被他们或微妙或野蛮粗暴地控制着；然而，"不去遵从"也仅仅是一种反抗权威的被动反应，它绝不可能帮助我们成为完整的人。反应是无穷无尽的，它只会导致进一步的反应。

遵从及其潜藏着的恐惧是一种障碍，然而仅仅在理智上认识到这个事实，是无法化解这个障碍的。只有当我们全身心地觉察到那些障碍时，我们才能摆脱它们而不再制造进一步和更深的阻碍。

The desire to imitate is a very strong factor in our life, not only at the superficial levels, but also profoundly. We have hardly any independent thoughts and feelings. When they do occur, they are mere reactions, and are therefore not free from the established pattern; for there is no freedom in reaction.

Philosophy and religion lay down certain methods whereby we can come to the realization of truth or God; yet merely to follow a method is to remain thoughtless and unintegrated, however beneficial the method may seem to be in our daily social life. The urge to conform, which is the desire for security, breeds fear and brings to the fore the political and religious authorities, the leaders and heroes who encourage subservience and by whom we are subtly or grossly dominated; but not to conform is only a reaction against authority, and in no way helps us to become integrated human beings. Reaction is endless, it only leads to further reaction.

Conformity, with its undercurrent of fear, is a hindrance; but intellectual recognition of this fact will not resolve the hindrance. It is only when we are aware of hindrances with our whole being that we can be free of them without creating further and deeper blockages.

当我们内心有所依赖时，传统就会牢牢地控制住我们，而一颗依照传统方式思考的心灵是无法发现新事物的。经由遵从，我们变成了平庸的模仿者和残酷的社会机器中的齿轮。我们自己的想法才是最重要的，而不是别人想要我们去想的东西。当我们遵从传统时，我们很快就变成了只是"我们应该怎样"的复制品。

这种对于"我们应该怎样"的模仿，滋生了恐惧，而恐惧扼杀了创造性的思考。恐惧使头脑和心灵变得迟钝，所以我们对生活的全部意义不再有所警觉；我们对自己的悲伤、鸟儿的飞翔、他人的笑容和苦难变得不再敏感。

意识层面和潜意识层面的恐惧，是由很多不同的原因所引起的，我们需要警觉留心，才能摆脱所有的恐惧。恐惧是无法通过克制、升华或者任何意志的行为来消除的，我们需要去寻找和了解它的根源。这需要耐心，以及一种不带有任何评判的觉察。

When we are inwardly dependent, then tradition has a great hold on us; and a mind that thinks along traditional lines cannot discover that which is new. By conforming we become mediocre imitators, cogs in a cruel social machine. It is what we think that matters, not what others want us to think. When we conform to tradition, we soon become mere copies of what we should be.

This imitation of what we should be, breeds fear; and fear kills thinking. Fear dulls the mind and heart so that we are not alert to the whole significance of life; we become insensitive to our own sorrows, to the movement of the birds, to the smiles and miseries of others.

Conscious and unconscious fear has many different causes, and alert watchfulness to be rid of them all. Fear cannot be eliminated through discipline, sublimation, or through any other act of will: its causes have to be searched out and understood. This needs patience and an awareness in which there is no judgment of any kind.

了解和消除我们意识层面的恐惧相对来说容易一些。然而对于潜意识层面的恐惧，我们大多数人甚至还未曾发现它们，因为我们不让它们浮出水面；当它们偶尔浮出水面时，我们就赶快把它们掩盖起来，逃避它们。潜藏着的各种恐惧常常会以梦境或其他形式的暗示来让我们知晓它们的存在，相较于意识表层的恐惧，它们导致了更大的退化和冲突。

我们的生活并不仅仅止于表面，它更巨大的部分由于我们疏于观察而被隐藏了起来。如果我们想让自己隐蔽的恐惧显露出来并且消除它，意识层面的头脑就必须多多少少安静下来，而不是一刻不停地忙碌着；然后，当这些恐惧浮出水面时，我们必须毫无阻碍地观察它们，因为任何形式的谴责或辩护都只会加强恐惧。要摆脱所有的恐惧，我们必须意识到它的负面影响，而只有持续不断的警觉才能揭示出造成恐惧的诸多原因。

It is comparatively easy to understand and dissolve our conscious fears. But unconscious fears are not even discovered by most of us, for we do not allow them to come to the surface; and when on rare occasions they do come to the surface, we hasten to cover them up, to escape from them. Hidden fears often make their presence known through dreams and other forms of intimation, and they cause greater deterioration and conflict than do the superficial fears.

Our lives are not just on the surface, their greater part is from casual observation. If we would have our obscure fears the open and dissolve, the conscious mind must be somewhat everlastingly occupied; then, as these fears come to the surface, be observed without let or hindrance, for any form of condemnation or justification only strengthens fear. To be free from all fear, we must be awake to its darkening influence, and only constant watchfulness can reveal its many causes.

恐惧所造成的结果之一,就是我们接受了人类事务中的权威。经由我们想要正确、安全、慰藉和免于意识层面冲突或困扰的渴望,我们制造了权威;然而任何源自恐惧的事物,都无法帮助我们了解自身的问题,尽管恐惧也许会表现为对那些所谓"智者"的尊敬和顺从。但智者是不会去行使权威的,那些权威人士都不是智者。任何形式的恐惧,都会妨碍我们了解自己以及我们与一切事物的关系。

跟从权威否定了智慧。接受权威就是服从于支配,让自己服从于某个人、某个团体、某种意识形态——不管是宗教上的还是政治上的;这种对权威的服从不仅否定了智慧,也否定了个体的自由。遵从某种教义或思想体系是一种自我防卫的反应。接受权威或许能帮助我们暂时地掩盖自己的困境和问题;然而回避一个问题只会加强它,在回避问题的过程中,我们也放弃了自我了解和自由。

One of the results of fear is the acceptance of authority in human affairs. Authority is created by our desire to be right, to be secure, to be comfortable, to have no conscious conflicts or disturbances; but nothing which results from fear can help us to understand our problems, even though fear may take the form of respect and submission to the so-called wise. The wise wield no authority, and those in authority are not wise. Fear in whatever form prevents the understanding of ourselves and of our relationship to all things.

The following of authority is the denial of intelligence. To accept authority is to submit to domination, to subjugate oneself to an to a group, or to an ideology, whether religious or political; subjugation of oneself to authority is the denial, not only of intelligence, but also of individual freedom. Compliance with a creed or a system of ideas is a self-protective reaction. The acceptance of authority may help us temporarily to cover up our difficulties and problems; but to avoid a problem is only to intensify it, and in the process, self-knowledge and freedom are abandoned.

自由和接受权威之间怎么可能存在妥协？如果存在妥协，那么那些声称自己在寻求自我了解和自由的人，就没有在认真地、尽全力地做这件事。我们似乎觉得自由是最终的目标，是一个终点，因此为了获得自由，我们必须首先让自己屈从于各种压制与恐吓。我们希望通过遵从来达到自由，难道手段不是和结果一样重要吗？难道不是手段造就了结果吗？

要拥有和平，我们就必须采用和平的手段来获得它，如果手段是暴力的，结果怎么可能是和平的？如果终点是自由，起点必须也是自由的，因为终点和起点是一体的。只有一开始就自由，才可能会有自我了解与智慧；然而，接受权威就否定了自由。

我们崇拜各式各样的权威：知识、成功、权力，等等。我们在年轻人身上行使权威，同时我们自己也害怕更高的权威。如果一个人自身没有内在的洞见，外在的权力和地位就会显得无比重要，于是，个体就越来越服从于权威和强制，就变成了别人手中的工具。

How can there be compromise between freedom and the acceptance of authority? If there is compromise, then those who say they are seeking self-knowledge and freedom are not earnest in their endeavour. We seem to think that freedom is an ultimate end, a goal, and that in order to become free we must first submit ourselves to various forms of suppression and intimidation. We hope to achieve freedom through conformity; but are not the means as important as the end? Do not the means shape the end?

To have peace, one must employ peaceful means; for if the violent, how can the end be peaceful? If the end is freedom, the beginning must be free, for the end and the beginning are one. There can be self-knowledge and intelligence only when there is freedom at the very outset; and freedom is denied by the acceptance of authority.

We worship authority in various forms: knowledge, success, power, and so on. We exert authority on the young, and at the same time we are afraid of superior authority. When man himself has no inward vision, outward power and position assume vast importance, and then the individual is more and more subject to authority and compulsion, he becomes the instrument of others.

如果我们能了解自己渴望支配或被支配背后的那股冲动，也许我们就能摆脱权威极其有害的影响了。我们渴望确定、渴望正确、渴望获得成功、渴望能够明白；而这种想要确定和永久的渴望，在我们心中建立起了个人经验的权威；而外在，它则制造了社会、家庭、宗教等权威。然而，仅仅去无视权威，去摆脱它那些外在的符号，也没有多大意义。

放弃一种传统，去遵从另一种传统；离开这个领袖，去跟随那个领袖——这些只不过是一种肤浅的姿态。如果我们想要觉察权威的整个运作过程，看清它的内在本质，以及了解和超越那种对确定的渴望，我们就必须有广泛的觉知和洞察，我们必须自由，不是在最后才自由，而是一开始就自由。

If we can understand the compulsion behind our desire to to be dominated, then perhaps we can be free from the crippling effects of authority. We crave to be certain, to be right, to be successful, to know; and this desire for certainty, for permanence, builds up within ourselves the authority of personal experience, while outwardly it creates the authority of society, of the family, of religion, and so on. But merely to ignore authority, to shake off its outward symbols, is of very little significance.

To break away from one tradition and conform to another, to leave this leader and follow that, is but a superficial gesture. If we are to be aware of the whole process of authority, if we are to see the inwardness of it, if we are to understand and transcend the desire for certainty, then we must have extensive awareness and insight, we must be free, not at the end, but at the beginning.

渴望确定、渴望安全——这是自我的主要活动之一，我们必须不断地观察这种强迫性的欲望，而不仅仅是扭转或强迫自己往另一个方向走，或者去遵从自己想要的某种模式。在我们大多数人身上，自我、"我"和"我的"都很强大；不管你是睡着了还是醒着，它时刻保持着警觉，总是在强化着自己。然而当有了对自我的觉察，并且意识到它所有的活动——不管多么微妙——都必然会带来冲突和痛苦时，对确定和自我延续的渴望就会结束。我们必须时时警惕自我，从而揭示出它的运作方式和"诡计"；不过，当我们开始了解它们，了解权威的含义，以及我们接受和否定权威中所蕴含着的一切意义时，我们就已经在让自己脱离权威了。

只要心灵还在允许自己被渴求自身安全的欲望支配和控制，它便无法从自我及其诸多问题中解脱出来；这就是我们经由教条和组织化的信仰——我们称之为宗教——无法从自我中解脱的原因。教条和信仰只不过是我们自己心灵的投射。仪式、普迦（普迦是印度教中向神祇膜拜的仪式——译者注）、那些公认的冥想方法、不断重复的某些咒语，虽然它们也许能产生一些令人满足的反应，却无法把心灵从自我及其活动中解放出来，因为自我本质上就是感觉的产物。

The craving for certainty, for security is one of the major activities of the self, and it is this compelling urge that has to be constantly watched, and not merely twisted or forced in another direction, or made to conform to a desired pattern. The self, the "me" and the "mine", is very strong in most of us; sleeping or waking, it is ever alert, always strengthening itself. But when there is an awareness of the self and a realization that all its activities, however subtle, must inevitably lead to conflict and pain, then the craving for certainty, for self-continuance comes to an end. One has to be constantly watchful for the self to reveal its ways and tricks; but when we begin to understand them, and to understand the implications of authority and all that is involved in our acceptance and denial of it, then we are already disentangling ourselves from authority.

As long as the mind allows itself to be dominated and controlled by the desire for its own security, there can be no release from the self problems; and that is why there is no release from the self and organized belief, which we call religion. Dogma and belief projections of our own mind. The rituals, the puja , the accepted forms of meditation, the constantly-repeated words and phrases, though they may produce certain gratifying responses, do not free the mind from the self and its activities; for the self is essentially the outcome of sensation.

在悲伤的时刻，我们会求助于我们的所谓上帝——他只不过是我们自己头脑制造的一个形象；或者我们会找到一些令人满意的解释，这些解释让我们获得了暂时的安慰。我们所追随的那些宗教，是我们经由自身的希望和恐惧，经由我们渴望内在的安全与保证所制造出来的，而伴随着对权威的崇拜——不管是救世主的权威、上师的权威还是牧师的权威——就出现了服从、接受和模仿。

不管我们以什么名字称呼自己，我们都是人类，而痛苦就是我们的宿命。我们所有人都会经历悲伤，不管是理想主义者还是唯物主义者。理想主义是对事实的逃避，而唯物主义则以另一种方式否定了深不可测的当下。两者都有他们自己回避痛苦这个复杂问题的方式；两者都被他们自身的渴望、野心和冲突消耗殆尽，他们的生活方式无助于心灵的平静。他们都需要对这个世界的混乱与不幸负责。

当我们处于冲突或痛苦中时，我们并未理解它们：在那种状态中，无论我们的行动或许经过了多么狡猾和仔细的慎重考虑，都只会导致更深的困惑和悲伤。要了解冲突从而摆脱它，就必须觉察到意识头脑和潜意识头脑的运作方式。

In moments of sorrow, we turn to what we call God, which is image of our own minds; or we find gratifying explanations, and this gives us temporary comfort. The religions that we follow are created by our hopes and fears, by our desire for inward security and reassurance; and with the worship of authority, whether it is that of a saviour, a master or a priest, there come submission, acceptance and imitation.

We are all human beings, by whatever name we may call ourselves, and suffering is our lot. Sorrow is common to all of us, to the idealist and to the materialist. Idealism is an escape from what is , and materialism is another way of denying the measureless depths of the present. Both the idealist and the materialist have their own ways of avoiding the complex problem of suffering; both are consumed by their own cravings, ambitions and conflicts, and their ways of life are not conducive to tranquillity. They are both responsible for the confusion and misery of the world.

Now, when we are in a state of conflict, of suffering, there is no comprehension: in that state, however cunningly and carefully thought out our action may be, it can only lead to further confusion and sorrow. To understand conflict and so to be free from it, there must be an awareness of the ways of the conscious and of the unconscious mind.

没有任何理想主义、体系或模式可以帮助我们揭示出心灵的深层活动；相反，任何公式或结论都会阻碍我们发现它们。追求"应该怎样"，执着于各种原则、理想，设定一个目标，这一切导致了诸多的幻想。如果我们想知晓自己，就必须有自发性，能够自由地去观察，然而当心灵封闭在肤浅的事物中，封闭在理想主义的价值观中时，这一切就不可能了。

生活就是关系。不管我们是否隶属于某个组织化的宗教，不管我们是世俗的还是沉浸在理想中，我们的痛苦都只能通过关系中的自我了解来加以解决。唯有自我了解才能给人类带来安宁和幸福，因为自我了解是智慧和完整的起点。智慧并不仅仅是表面的调整适应，它不只是培育心智和获取知识。智慧是有能力去了解生活的方方面面，它是对正确价值的洞察。

No idealism, no system or pattern of any kind, can help us to unravel the deep workings of the mind; on the contrary, any formulation or conclusion will hinder their discovery. The pursuit of what should be, the attachment to principles, to ideals, the establishment of a goal — all this leads to many illusions. If we are to know ourselves, there must be a certain spontaneity, a freedom to observe, and this is not possible when the mind is enclosed in the superficial, in idealistic values.

Existence is relationship; and whether we belong to an organized religion or not, whether we are worldly or caught up in ideals, our suffering can be resolved only through the understanding of ourselves in relationship. Self-knowledge alone can bring tranquillity and happiness to man, for self-knowledge is the beginning of intelligence and integration. Intelligence is not mere superficial adjustment; it is not the cultivation of the mind, the acquisition of knowledge. Intelligence is the capacity to understand the ways of life, it is the perception of right values.

现代教育在开发智力的过程中，提供了越来越多的理论和事实，却没能让我们了解人类存在的整体过程。我们的智力高度发展，我们已经培养了灵活的头脑，沉浸在无数的解释中。智力会满足于理论和解释，但智慧不会，而要了解生活的整体过程，我们的行动中就必须要有头脑和心灵的融合。智慧和爱是不可分割的。

对我们大多数人而言，要实现这种内在的革命是极其艰难的。我们知道如何冥想、如何弹奏钢琴、如何写作，然而，对那个冥想者、弹奏者和写作者，我们却一无所知。我们并不是创造者，因为我们已经用知识、信息和傲慢填满了我们的心灵和头脑；我们内心充满了对别人思想或话语的引用。然而首要的是体验，而不是体验的方式。在能够表达爱之前，必须先要有爱。

Modern education, in developing the intellect, offers more and more theories and facts, without bringing about the understanding of the total process of human existence. We are highly intellectual; we have developed cunning minds, and are caught up in explanations. The intellect is satisfied with theories and explanations, but intelligence is not; and for the understanding of the total process of existence, there must be an integration of the mind and heart in action. Intelligence is not separate from love.

For most of us, to accomplish this inward revolution is extremely arduous. We know how to meditate, how to play the piano, how to write, but we have no knowledge of the meditator, the player, the writer. We are not creators, for we have filled our hearts and minds with knowledge, information and arrogance; we are full of quotations from what others have thought or said. But experiencing comes first, not the way of experiencing. There must be love before there can be the expression of love.

所以很清楚的一点就是，仅仅培育智力——也就是发展能力或知识——不会带来智慧。智力和智慧是有区别的。智力是脱离情感的思想的运作，而智慧则是将感受与理性融为一体的能力；除非我们能以智慧去面对生活，而不仅仅是以智力或情感去处理它，否则世界上任何的政治或教育体系，都无法把我们从这种混乱和毁灭的罗网中解救出来。

知识无法与智慧相比，知识不是智慧。智慧是无法买卖的，它不是一件可以通过付出学习或训练的代价而"买"到的商品。智慧无法在书本中找到，你无法积累、记住或储存它。智慧伴随着对自我的舍弃而来。拥有一颗开放的心灵远远比学习更重要；要拥有一颗开放的心灵，就不能让心灵塞满各种信息，而应该去觉察我们自身的思想和感受；去细心地观察我们自己，以及我们周围的各种影响；去聆听他人的话语；去观察富人和穷人、有权有势者和弱势群体。智慧不是通过恐惧和压迫产生的，而是通过观察和了解人类关系中的日常事件到来的。

It is clear, then, that merely to cultivate the intellect, which is to develop capacity or knowledge, does not result in intelligence. There is a distinction between intellect and intelligence. Intellect is thought functioning independently of emotion, whereas, intelligence is the capacity to feel as well as to reason; and until we approach life with intelligence, instead of intellect alone, or with emotion alone, no political or educational system in the world can save us from the toils of chaos and destruction.

Knowledge is not comparable with intelligence, knowledge is not wisdom. Wisdom is not marketable, it is not a merchandise that can be bought with the price of learning or discipline. Wisdom cannot be found in books; it cannot be accumulated, memorized or stored up. Wisdom comes with the abnegation of the self. To have an open mind is more important than learning; and we can have an open mind, not by cramming it full of information, but by being aware of our own thoughts and feelings, by carefully observing ourselves and the influences about us, by listening to others, by watching the rich and the poor, the powerful and the lowly. Wisdom does not come through fear and oppression, but through the observation and understanding of everyday incidents in human relationship.

在我们寻求知识的过程中，在我们贪得无厌的欲望中，我们失去了爱，我们对美的感受和对残忍的敏感性变得迟钝了；我们变得越来越专业化，也越来越不完整。智慧无法用知识来替代，无论多少解释，无论积累多少资讯，都无法让人类从痛苦中解脱出来。知识是必需的，科学也有它的位置，然而如果头脑和心灵被知识扼制，如果我们用一些解释就把痛苦的原因给糊弄过去了，那么生活就会变得空虚且毫无意义。这难道不是发生在我们大多数人身上的事吗？我们的教育正把我们变得越来越肤浅，它并没有帮助我们揭示出我们存在中更深的层面，我们的生活正变得越来越空虚。

虽然信息和关于各类事实的知识在不断增长，但它本质上还是有限的。而智慧是无限的，它既包含了知识，也包含了行为的方式；但我们只抓住了一根树枝，却认为它就是整棵大树。经由片面、局部的知识，我们永远无法了悟"整体"的喜悦。智力永远无法带领我们达到整体，因为它只不过是一个片段、一个部分。

In our search for knowledge, in our acquisitive desires, we are losing love, we are blunting the feeling for beauty, the sensitivity to cruelty; we are becoming more and more specialized and less integrated. Wisdom cannot be replaced by knowledge, and no of explanation, no accumulation of facts, will free man from Knowledge is necessary, science has its place; but if the mind and suffocated by knowledge, and if the cause of suffering is life becomes vain and meaningless. And is this not what is most of us? Our education is making us more and more shallow; it is not helping us to uncover the deeper layers of our being, and our lives are increasingly empty.

Information, the knowledge of facts, though ever increasing, is by its very nature limited. Wisdom is infinite, it includes knowledge and the action; but we take hold of a branch and think it is the whole tree. Through the knowledge of the part, we can never realize the joy of the whole. Intellect can never lead to the whole, for it is only a segment, a part.

我们已经把智力和感受分开了,并以牺牲感受为代价发展了智力。我们就像一个三条腿的物体,其中一条腿要远远长于另外两条,所以我们失去了平衡。我们被培养成理性的人,我们的教育培养了敏锐、狡猾和贪得无厌的智力,因此智力在我们的生活中扮演着一个无比重要的角色。智慧远远比智力更伟大,因为它是理性与爱的融合,然而只有自我了解,深刻理解了自己的全部过程时,智慧才会产生。

对人类来说——不管是年轻人还是老人——最重要的就是去充分地、完整地生活,这就是为什么我们主要的问题是要培养那种使人变得完整的智慧。过分强调我们整体结构中的任何一个组成部分,只会带来一种片面而扭曲的人生观,正是这种扭曲导致了我们大多数的难题。片面地发展我们整体性格中的任何一个部分,对我们自己和社会来说都注定是灾难性的,所以我们要带着一种整体观去处理我们人类的问题,这一点真的非常重要。

We have separated intellect from feeling, and have developed at the expense of feeling. We are like a three-legged object with one leg much longer than the others, and we have no balance. We are trained to be intellectual; our education cultivates the intellect to be sharp, cunning, acquisitive, and so it plays the most important role in our life. Intelligence is much greater than intellect, for it is the integration of reason but there can be intelligence only when there is self-knowledge, the deep understanding of the total process of oneself.

What is essential for man, whether young or old, is to live fully, integrally, and that is why our major problem is the cultivation of that intelligence which brings integration. Undue emphasis on any part of our total make- up gives a partial and therefore distorted view of life, and it is this distortion which is causing most of our difficulties. Any partial development of our whole temperament is bound to be disastrous both for ourselves and for society, and so it is really very important that we approach our human problems with an integrated point of view.

成为一个完整的人,就是去了解我们自身意识的整个过程——既包括潜藏的意识,也包括表面的意识。但如果我们过分强调智性,这一切就不可能了。我们无比重视头脑的培养,然而我们的内心是不足、贫乏与混乱的。依靠智性生活就是死路一条,因为思想观念就和信仰一样,是永远无法把人类团结起来的——除了把他们划分成彼此冲突的团体。

只要我们仍然依赖思想,把它作为一种达到完整的手段,就一定会有分裂,而了解思想分裂性的行为,就是去觉察自我的运作方式,以及我们自身欲望的运作方式。我们必须意识到我们的局限和它所产生的反应——既包括集体性的反应,也包括个人的反应。只有当我们充分觉察到自我的活动,以及它自相矛盾的欲望和追求,觉察到自我的各种希望与恐惧时,才有可能超越自我。

To be an integrated human being is to understand the entire one's own consciousness, both the hidden and the open. This is not possible if we give undue emphasis to the intellect. We attach great importance to the cultivation of the mind, but inwardly we are insufficient, poor and confused. This living in the intellect is the way of disintegration; for ideas, like beliefs, can never bring people together except in conflicting groups.

As long as we depend on thought as a means of integration, there must be disintegration; and to understand the disintegrating action of thought is to be aware of the ways of the self, the ways of one's own desire. We must be aware of our conditioning and its responses, both collective and personal. It is only when one is fully aware of the activities of the self with its contradictory desires and pursuits, its hopes and fears, that there is a possibility of going beyond the self.

唯有爱和正确的思考才能带来真正的革命——我们内心的革命。可是我们要如何才能拥有爱？不是通过追求爱的理想，而是当没有了仇恨、贪婪，当自我感——自我是造成对立的根源——止息时，只有那时我们才能拥有爱。一个沉浸在剥削、贪婪和妒忌中的人是永远无法去爱的。

没有爱和正确的思考，压迫和残酷就会不断增长。要解决人类互相对立的问题，并不是通过追求和平的理想，而是通过了解造成战争的原因——原因就存在于我们对待生活、对待同伴的态度中；而这种了解只有通过正确的教育才会产生。没有心灵的改变、没有善意、没有内在的转变——这种转变来自自我觉察——就不会有人类的和平与幸福。

Only love and right thinking will bring about true revolution, the revolution within ourselves. But how are we to have love? Not through the pursuit of the ideal of love, but only when there is no hatred, when there is no greed, when the sense of self, which is the cause of antagonism, comes to an end. A man who is caught up in the pursuits of exploitation, of greed, of envy, can never love.

Without love and right thinking, oppression and cruelty will ever be on the increase. The problem of man's antagonism to man can be solved, not by pursuing the ideal of peace, but by understanding the causes of war which lie in our attitude towards life, towards our fellow beings; and this understanding can come about only through the right kind of education. Without a change of heart, without goodwill, without the inward transformation which is born of self-awareness, there can be no peace, no happiness for men.

第四章

教育与世界和平

CHAPTER IV
EDUCATION AND WORLD PEACE

要发现教育在当今世界的危机中能够起到什么样的作用，我们就应该了解危机是如何产生的。很显然，它是由我们和他人、和财产、和观念的关系中错误的价值观所引起的。如果我们和他人的关系建立在自我扩张之上，如果我们对财产贪得无厌，那么这个社会的结构就必然是竞争性的、自我孤立的。如果在我们和观念的关系中，我们为某种意识形态辩护，同时反对另一种意识形态，那么就不可避免地会产生彼此之间的不信任和敌意了。

造成当今世界种种混乱的另一个原因，就是对权威的依赖——不管是在日常生活中，在小学里，还是在大学里。在任何一种文明中，权威都是导致堕落退化的因素。当我们跟从别人时，我们并没有任何了解，有的只是恐惧和遵从。

只要我们仍旧接受这种社会秩序，其中有着人与人之间无止境的斗争和对立，就不可能会有持久的幸福。如果我们想要改变现有的状况，我们就必须首先转变自己，这意味着我们必须觉察自己在日常生活中的行动、思想和感受。

To discover what part education can play in the present world should understand how that crisis has come into being. It is result of wrong values in our relationship to people, to property and to ideas. If our relationship with others is based on self-aggrandizement, and our relationship to property is acquisitive, the structure of society is bound to be competitive and self-isolating. If in our relationship with ideas we justify one ideology in opposition to another, mutual distrust and ill will are the inevitable results.

Another cause of the present chaos is dependence on authority, whether in daily life, in the small school or in the university. Authority are deteriorating factors in any culture. When we follow another there is no understanding, but only fear and conformity.

There can be no lasting happiness as long as we accept a social order in which there is endless strife and antagonism between man and man. If we want to change existing conditions, we must first transform ourselves, which means that we must become aware of our own actions, thoughts and feelings in everyday life.

但我们并不是真的想要和平,我们并不想停止剥削。我们不允许自己的贪婪受到干扰或者我们现有社会结构的基础遭到改变。我们想让一切照旧,最多只是进行一些表面的小修小改。于是,那些有权有势者和狡诈之人便不可避免地主宰了我们的生活。

和平无法借由任何意识形态而获得,它也不依赖于任何立法;只有当我们作为个体开始了解我们自身的心理过程时,和平才会降临。如果我们逃避了个人行动的责任,然后等待某种新的体系来建立和平的话,我们就只会成为那个体系的奴隶。

当政府、大财团和掌握教会大权的人,开始发现人类之间这种不断增长的对立只会导致大家同归于尽,从而不再有利可图时,他们或许就会通过立法和其他强制手段来迫使我们压抑个人的渴望和野心,然后通力合作来谋求人类的利益。就像我们现在被教育和鼓励着去变得富有竞争性和冷酷无情一样,那个时候我们将被迫去彼此尊重,然后去为整个世界的利益而工作。

But we do not really want peace, we do not want to put an exploitation. We will not allow our greed to be interfered with, foundations of our present social structure to be altered; we want things to continue as they are with only superficial modifications, and so the powerful, the cunning inevitably rule our lives.

Peace is not achieved through any ideology, it does not legislation; it comes only when we as individuals begin to understand our own psychological process. If we avoid the responsibility of acting individually and wait for some new system to establish peace, we shall merely become the slaves of that system.

When governments, big business and the clerically powerful begin to see that this increasing antagonism between men only leads to indiscriminate destruction and is therefore no longer profitable, they may force us, through legislation and other means of compulsion, to suppress our personal cravings and ambitions and to cooperate for the well-being of mankind. Just as we are now educated and encouraged to be competitive and ruthless, so then we shall be compelled to respect one another and to work for the world as a whole.

即使我们的衣食住行都无忧了，我们仍摆脱不了我们的冲突和敌意——它们只是转移到了另一个层面，在那里它们会变得更可怕、更具毁灭性。唯一道德的或正直的行为是自发的，而唯有了解才能给人类带来和平与幸福。

信仰、意识形态和组织化的宗教使我们去对抗我们的邻居；冲突不仅存在于不同的社会之间，同样存在于同一社会中的不同团体之间。我们必须意识到，只要我们还是执着于安全感，只要我们还是被教条制约，我们的内心和这个世界就仍将会有斗争和痛苦。

宗教组织以及它们世俗或精神上的权威，同样无法给人类带来和平，因为它们也是我们无知、恐惧、虚假和自我中心的产物。

And even though we may all be well fed, clothed and sheltered, we shall not be free of our conflicts and antagonisms, which will merely have shifted to another plane, where they will be still more diabolical and devastating. The only moral or righteous action is voluntary, and understanding alone can bring peace and happiness to man.

Beliefs, ideologies and organized religions are setting us against our neighbours; there is conflict, not only among different societies, but among groups within the same society. We must realize that as long as we cling to security, as long as we are conditioned by dogmas, there will be strife and misery both within ourselves and in the world.

Organized religions, with their temporal and spiritual authority, are equally incapable of bringing peace to man, for they also are the outcome of our ignorance and fear, of our make-believe and egotism.

由于渴望今生或来世的安全,我们建造出了保障这种安全感的制度和意识形态;然而,我们越是奋力追求安全感,我们的安全就越少。渴望安全只会助长分裂、增强对立。如果我们深刻感受到并理解了其中的真相——不仅是口头或智力上的,而是用我们全部的存在理解了——那么我们就可以在我们周围这个最近的世界里,开始从根本上去转变我们与我们同伴的关系;只有这样,才可能实现人类的团结和兄弟情谊。

我们大多数人都已被各种恐惧折磨得筋疲力尽,因此我们非常关心自身的安全。我们希望天降奇迹,让战争停止,我们一直在指控其他国家的群体是战争的煽动者——就像他们反过来指责是我们带来了灾难一样。虽然战争很显然是有害于社会的,我们却在为战争做准备,并且培养年轻人的军事精神。

Craving security here or in the hereafter, we create ideologies which guarantee that security; but the more we security, the less we shall have it. The desire to be secure only fosters division and increases antagonism. If we deeply feel and understand the truth of this, not merely verbally or intellectually, but with our whole being, then we shall begin to alter fundamentally our relationship with our fellow men in the immediate world about us; and only then is there a possibility of achieving unity and brotherhood.

Most of us are consumed by all sorts of fears, and are greatly concerned about our own security. We hope that, by some miracle, wars will come to an end, all the while accusing other national groups of being the instigators of war, as they in turn blame us for the disaster. Although war is so obviously detrimental to society, we prepare for war and develop in the young the military spirit.

如果我们的生活带来的只是我们内心以及我们和他人之间无止境的冲突，如果我们渴望让流血牺牲和痛苦永远存在下去，那么就必须有更多的士兵、更多的政客、更多的仇恨——而这就是实际在发生的事。现代文明是基于暴力的，因此它招来了死亡。只要我们还崇尚武力，暴力便会成为我们的生活方式。但如果我们想要和平，如果我们想要人与人之间有正确的关系——不管是基督教徒与印度教徒之间，还是俄国人与美国人之间——如果我们想让自己的孩子成为完整的人，那么军事训练就绝对是一道障碍，开始这种训练就是误入歧途。

仇恨和斗争的主要原因之一，就是人们相信某个阶层或民族要比另一个更优秀。孩子既没有阶级意识，也没有民族意识；是家庭、学校或者两者皆有的环境让他感觉到了那种分别。在他心里，他并不在乎他的玩伴是黑人还是犹太人，是婆罗门还是非婆罗门；然而整个社会结构所造成的影响在不断地冲击着他的心灵，影响并塑造着它。

这里的问题同样不在于孩子，而在于大人，是大人建造出了一个充满分裂和错误价值的愚蠢环境。

If we are living only to have endless strife within ourselves others, if our desire is to perpetuate bloodshed and misery, then there must be more soldiers, more politicians, more enmity — which is what is actually happening. Modern civilization is based on violence, and is therefore courting death. As long as we worship force, violence will be our way of life. But if we want peace, if we want right relationship among men, whether Christian or Hindu, Russian or American, if we want our children to be integrated human beings, then military training is an absolute hindrance, it is the wrong way to set about it.

One of the chief causes of hatred and strife is the belief that a particular class or race is superior to another. The child is neither class nor race conscious; it is the home or school environment, or both, which makes him feel separative. In himself he does not care whether his playmate is a Negro or a Jew, a Brahmin or a non-Brahmin; but the influence of the whole social structure is continually impinging on his mind, affecting and shaping it.

Here again the problem is not with the child but with the adults, who have created a senseless environment of separatism and false values.

区分人类的真正依据是什么？我们的身体结构和肤色也许不同，我们的相貌也许不一样，然而在皮肤底下的我们是非常相似的：骄傲、野心勃勃、妒忌、暴力、充满性欲、追逐权力，等等。拿掉那些标签，我们都是赤裸裸的一无所有，但我们并不想去面对我们的赤裸，于是我们坚持保留那些标签——这表明了我们是多么的不成熟，多么的幼稚。

要使孩子能够免于偏见地成长，我们就必须首先打破自己内心所有的偏见，然后打破存在于自己周围的所有偏见——这意味着去打破我们所建造出来的这种毫无思考的社会结构。在家里，我们也许会告诉孩子，阶级或民族意识是多么荒谬，而他可能也会赞同我们；然而，当他去学校和其他小孩玩耍的时候，他就会被那种划分人类的态度污染。或者反过来：家庭也许是传统的、狭隘的，而学校则更开放、包容一些。然而不管哪种情况，家庭环境和学校环境之间都会存在不停的斗争，而小孩则被困在两者之间。

What real basis is there for differentiating between human bodies may be different in structure and colour, our faces may be dissimilar, but inside the skin we are very much alike: proud, ambitious, violent, sexual, power-seeking and so on. Remove the label and we are very naked; but we do not want to face our nakedness, and so we insist on the label — which indicates how immature, how really infantile we are.

To enable the child to grow up free from prejudice, one has first to break down all prejudice within oneself, and then in one's environment — which means breaking down the structure of this thoughtless society which we have created. At home we may tell the child how absurd it is to be conscious of one's class or race, and he will probably agree with us; but when he goes to school and plays with other children, he becomes contaminated by the separative spirit. Or it may be the other way around: the home may be traditional, narrow, and the school's influence may be broader. In either case there is a constant battle between the home and the school environments, and the child is caught between the two.

要让孩子心智健全地成长,要帮助孩子去觉察,从而使他识破那些愚蠢的偏见,我们就必须和他保持亲密的关系。我们必须充分地讨论各种主题,让他在一旁聆听这些智慧的对话;我们必须鼓励他们内心本来就存在的探寻精神和不满之情,通过这种方式去帮助他,让他自己去发现什么是正确的,什么是错误的。

持续不断的探寻和真正的不满之情,带来了创造性的智慧;然而要让探寻和不满一直保持觉醒是极其费力的,大多数人并不想让他们的孩子拥有这种智慧。

年轻的时候我们都是不满的,但不幸的是我们的不满很快就消退了,我们身上模仿的倾向和对权威的崇拜抑制了这种不满。当我们年纪稍微大一点以后,我们开始变得僵化,变得容易心满意足、胆小怕事。我们成了主管、教士、银行职员、工厂经理、技术人员,然后便逐渐开始腐朽了。因为我们想要保住自己的位置,于是我们便去支持这个具有毁灭性的社会——是它把我们送上了那个位置,并且给予了我们某种程度的安全感。

To raise a child sanely, to help him to be perceptive so that he sees through these stupid prejudices, we have to be in close relationship with him. We have to talk things over and let him listen to intelligent conversation; we have to encourage the spirit of inquiry and discontent which is already in him, thereby helping him to discover for himself what is true and what is false.

It is constant inquiry, true dissatisfaction, that brings creative intelligence; but to keep inquiry and discontent awake is extremely arduous, and most people do not want their children to have this kind of intelligence.

All of us are discontented when we are young, but discontent soon fades away, smothered by our imitative tendencies and our worship of authority. As we grow older, we begin to crystallize, to be satisfied and apprehensive. We become executives, priests, bank clerks, factory managers, technicians, and slow decay sets in. Because we desire to maintain our positions, we support the destructive society which has placed us there and given us some measure of security.

如果你待在你的国家，我待在我的国家，保持着我们各自的宗教偏见和经济运转方式，我们又如何能成为和平相处的人类呢？只要爱国主义还在划分着人类，只要成千上万的人还受困于萧条的经济状况中，而同时其他国家的人却生活富裕，我们又怎么可能会有兄弟情谊呢？当各种信仰在分裂着我们时，当某个团体在支配另一个团体时，当富人们有权有势，而穷人也在谋求同样的权力时，当土地分配不公时，当一些人饱餐而多数人却在挨饿时，又怎么会有人类的团结呢？

我们的困难之一，在于我们并没有真的对这些事情认真，因为我们不想受到太大干扰。我们更喜欢以一种对自己有利的方式来改变事物，所以我们并没有深刻地去关注我们自身的空虚和残忍。

How can we get together as human beings if you in your country, and I in mine, retain our respective religious prejudices and economic ways? How can there be brotherhood as long as millions are restricted by depressed economic conditions while others are well off? How can there be human unity when beliefs divide us, when there is domination of one group by another, when the rich are powerful and the poor are seeking that same power, when there is maldistribution of land, when some are well fed and multitudes are starving?

One of our difficulties is that we are not really in earnest matters, because we do not want to be greatly disturbed. We prefer to alter things only in a manner advantageous to ourselves, and so we are not deeply concerned about our own emptiness and cruelty.

我们可能通过暴力来达到和平吗？和平是通过缓慢的时间过程来逐渐达到的吗？显然，爱和训练或时间无关。我相信上两次世界大战是为了争取民主，而现在，我们正在准备一场规模更浩大、更具毁灭性的战争，而人民却比以往更缺乏自由。然而，如果我们可以把这些阻止了解的明显障碍——比如权威、信仰和整个阶级划分的态度——扔到一边，那么会发生什么？我们将会成为没有权威的人类，人类彼此之间将会产生直接的关系——到了那时，也许就会有爱与慈悲了。

在教育领域——就像在其他领域中一样——最重要的就是要找到一些通情达理并且满怀关爱的人，这些人的心灵不会充斥着空洞的话语和头脑所制造的事物。

如果生活意味着带着思考、关怀与爱去快乐地活着，那么了解我们自己就非常重要；如果我们希望建立一个真正开明的社会，就必须要有一些了解达到完整的途径的教育者，由此他们就能够把那份了解传递给孩子。

Can we ever attain peace through violence? Is peace to be achieved gradually, through a slow process of time? Surely, love is not a matter of training or of time. The last two wars were fought for democracy, I believe; and now we are preparing for a still greater and more destructive war, and people are less free. But what would happen if we were to put aside such obvious hindrances to understanding as authority, belief and the whole hierarchical spirit? We would be people without authority, human beings in direct relationship with one another — and then, perhaps, there would be love and compassion.

What is essential in education, as in every other field, is to who are understanding and affectionate, whose hearts are not empty phrases, with the things of the mind.

If life is meant to be lived happily, with thought, with care, with affection, then it is very important to understand ourselves; and if we wish to build a truly enlightened society, we must have educators who understand the ways of integration and who are therefore capable of imparting that understanding to the child.

这种教育者将会威胁到如今的社会结构。然而，我们并没有真正想去建立一个开明的社会；一个老师，如果他理解了和平的全部含义，从而开始指出战争的愚蠢，那么他很快就会丢掉职位。明白了这一点以后，大多数老师选择了妥协。

毫无疑问，要发现真理，我们就必须摆脱冲突——既包括我们内心的冲突，也包括我们和邻居的冲突。当我们内在没有了冲突，就不会有外在的冲突。正是内在的冲突向外投射，才演变成了世界上的冲突。战争就是我们日常生活浩大而血腥的投射。我们经由自己每天的生活而促成了战争；没有我们内在的转变，就必定会有国家和种族的对立、关于不同意识形态的幼稚争论、不断地扩充军队、向旗帜致敬，以及所有那些制造出有组织的屠杀的残忍无情。

Such educators would be a danger to the present structure of society. But we do not really want to build an enlightened society; and any teacher who, perceiving the full implications of peace, began to point out the stupidity of war, would soon lose his position. Knowing this, most teachers compromise.

Surely, to discover truth, there must be freedom from strife, both within ourselves and with our neighbours. When we are not in conflict within ourselves, we are not in conflict outwardly. It is the inward strife which, projected outwardly, becomes the world conflict. War is the spectacular and bloody projection of our everyday living. We precipitate war out of our daily lives; and without a transformation in ourselves, there are bound to be national and racial antagonisms, the childish quarrelling over ideologies, the multiplication of soldiers, the saluting of flags, and all the many brutalities that go to create organized murder.

政府正在训练年轻人成为他们所需的高效率的军人和技术人员；他们培育和强制执行纪律与偏见。考虑到这些事实后，我们必须去探究我们存在的含义，以及我们生活的意义和目的。我们必须找到一些有益的方式来创造一个新的环境，因为环境可以把孩子变成一个禽兽、一个冷酷无情的专家，也可以帮助孩子成为一个敏感、智慧的人。

这一切意味着去了解存在于我们关系中的彼此之间的责任；但要了解我们的责任，我们内心就必须有爱，而不仅仅是只有学问或知识。我们的爱越强烈，对社会的影响就越深远。但我们都只有头脑，没有心灵；我们培养智力，却鄙视谦卑。如果我们真的爱自己的孩子，我们就会设法挽救和保护他们，不会让他们战死沙场。

我认为我们渴望武器，我们喜欢展示军事力量、制服、仪式、酒精、喧闹、暴力。我们每天的生活就是这些可恶的肤浅之事的缩影，由于妒忌和缺乏思考，我们正在互相毁灭。

Governments are training the young to be the efficient soldiers and technicians they need; regimentation and prejudice are being cultivated and enforced. Taking these facts into consideration, we have to inquire into the meaning of existence and the significance and purpose of our lives. We have to discover the beneficent ways of creating a new environment; for environment can make the child a brute, an unfeeling specialist, or help him to become a sensitive, intelligent human being.

All this implies the understanding of our responsibility to one another in relationship; but to understand our responsibility, there must be love in our hearts, not mere learning or knowledge. The greater our love, the deeper will be its influence on society. But we are all brains and no heart; we cultivate the intellect and despise humility. If we really loved our children, we would want to save and protect them, we would not let them be sacrificed in wars.

I think we really want arms; we like the show of military power, the uniforms, the rituals, the drinks, the noise, the violence. Our everyday life is a reflection in miniature of this same brutal superficiality, and we are destroying one another through envy and thoughtlessness.

我们想变得富有，而我们越是富有，就越冷酷无情——尽管我们也许会捐一大笔钱给慈善机构和教育机构。在掠夺了受害人以后，我们还给他一点点赃物——我们就把这称为慈善。我认为我们并没有意识到自己正在准备着一场多么可怕的灾难。我们大多数人都在尽可能匆忙和毫无思考地度过每一天，同时把我们生活的方向交给政府和狡猾的政客去处理。

所有的主权政府都必然会为战争做准备，我们自己的政府也不例外。要让它的国民骁勇善战，要让他们准备好去高效地履行职责，政府很显然必须控制和支配他们。他们必须被教育得像机器那样去行动，拥有冷酷无情的高效率。如果生活的目的和终点是去毁灭或者被毁灭，那么教育就必须去鼓励残忍无情——而我完全无法确定这不是我们内心所期望的东西，因为残忍无情总是会伴随着对成功的崇拜。

We want to be rich; and the richer we get, the more ruthless we become, even though we may contribute large sums to charity and education. Having robbed the victim, we return to him a little of the spoils, and this we call philanthropy. I do not think we realize what catastrophes we are preparing. Most of us live each day as rapidly and thoughtlessly as possible, and leave to the governments, to the cunning politicians, the direction of our lives.

All sovereign governments must prepare for war, and one's own government is no exception. To make its citizens efficient for war, to prepare them to perform their duties effectively, the government must obviously control and dominate them. They must be educated to act as machines, to be ruthlessly efficient. If the purpose and end of life is to destroy or be destroyed, then education must encourage ruthlessness; and I am not at all sure that that is not what we inwardly desire, for ruthlessness goes with the worship of success.

另一方面，也有一些人在设法掀起暴力革命。在帮助建立起了现有的社会秩序及其所有的冲突、混乱和痛苦以后，现在他们渴望去组建一个完美的社会。然而当我们自己就是如今这个社会的始作俑者时，我们中还有人能组建一个完美的社会吗？相信和平可以通过暴力来实现，就是在为了未来的理想而牺牲现在。通过错误的手段来谋求正确的结果——这就是造成当今灾难的原因之一。

感官价值的膨胀和凸显阻止了人与人之间的合作，腐化了人类的关系——人类的关系就是社会。社会就是你和他人之间的关系，没有深刻地了解这种关系——不是任何单一层面上的了解，而是完整地、整体性地去了解它——我们必定会再次建立同样的社会结构，不管它表面上有多大的改进。

On the other hand, there are those who seek to bring about a revolution. Having helped to build the existing social order conflicts, confusion and misery, they now desire to organize a perfect society. But can any of us organize a perfect society when it is we who have brought into being the present one? To believe that peace can be achieved through violence is to sacrifice the present for a future ideal; and this seeking of a right end through wrong means is one of the causes of the present disaster.

The expansion and predominance of sensate values exclude man's cooperation with man and corrupts human relationship, which is society. Society is the relationship between you and another; and without deeply understanding this relationship, not at any one level, but integrally, as a total process, we are bound to create again the same kind of social structure, however superficially modified.

如果我们想要彻底改变如今的人类关系——这种关系给这个世界带来了无尽的痛苦——那么我们唯一的、紧迫的任务就是通过自我了解去转变我们自己。所以我们回到了核心问题上，也就是我们自己；然而，我们却回避了这一点，然后把责任转嫁给了政府、宗教和各种意识形态。政府就是我们自己，宗教和意识形态只不过是我们自身的一种投射；所以除非我们有了根本的改变，否则既不会有正确的教育，也不会有和平的世界。

只有具备了爱与智慧，所有人外在的安全才会降临；由于我们已经建造了一个充满冲突与不幸的世界——在其中所有人的外在安全正在迅速地变为不可能——这难道不是表明了我们过去和现在的教育是彻底无用的吗？作为父母和老师，我们最直接的责任就是去打破那些传统的思维，而不仅仅是依靠专家和他们的发现。技术上的高效率使我们有了某种赚钱的能力，这就是大多数人满足于现有社会结构的原因；然而真正的教育者只关心正确的生活、正确的教育和正确的谋生之道。

If we are to change radically our present human relationship, which has brought untold misery to the world, our only and immediate task is to transform ourselves through self-knowledge. So we come back to the central point, which is oneself; but we dodge that point and shift the responsibility onto governments, religions and ideologies. The government is what we are, religions and ideologies are but a projection of ourselves; and until we change fundamentally there can be neither right education nor a peaceful world.

Outward security for all can come only when there is love and intelligence; and since we have created a world of conflict and misery in which outward security is rapidly becoming impossible for anyone, does it not indicate the utter futility of past and present education? As parents and teachers it is our direct responsibility to break away from traditional thinking, and not merely rely on the experts and their findings. Efficiency in technique has given us a certain capacity to earn money, and that is why most of us are satisfied with the present social structure; but the true educator is concerned only with right living, right education, and right means of livelihood.

另一场更大的灾难已经迫在眉睫了，而我们大多数人依然对此毫无行动。我们仍然和从前一样地度过一天又一天，我们并不想除去我们所有错误的价值然后重新开始。我们想要进行一些小修小补的改革——这种改革只会导致一些需要进一步改革的问题。然而大楼正在瓦解，墙壁正在倒塌，大火正在烧毁它。我们必须离开那幢大楼，然后在一片新的土地上，以一种完全不同的基础和价值重新建造。

我们不能抛弃技术知识，但我们可以从内在觉察到我们的丑陋、无情、欺骗、不诚实以及爱的彻底缺乏。只有通过把我们自己从妒忌和对权力的渴望中智慧地解脱出来，我们才能建立起一种新的社会秩序。

和平无法通过小修小补的改革来达成，也无法仅仅通过重新整理旧有的观念和迷信来获得。只有当我们了解了那超越肤浅表面的事物，从而制止了毁灭的洪流时——这股洪流是经由我们自身的侵略性和恐惧所释放出来的——才会有和平。

Another and still greater disaster is approaching dangerously most of us are doing nothing whatever about it. We go on day exactly as before; we do not want to strip away all our false values and begin anew. We want to do patchwork reform, which only leads to problems of still further reform. But the building is crumbling, the walls are giving way, and fire is destroying it. We must leave the building and start on new ground, with different foundations, different values.

We cannot discard technical knowledge, but we can become inwardly aware of our ugliness, of our ruthlessness, of our deceptions and dishonesty, our utter lack of love. Only by intelligently freeing ourselves, from envy and the thirst for power, can a new social order be established.

Peace is not to be achieved by patchwork reform, nor by a mere rearrangement of old ideas and superstitions. There can be when we understand what lies beyond the superficial, and thereby stop this wave of destruction which has been unleashed by our own aggressiveness and fears.

第五章

学校

CHAPTER V

THE SCHOOL

正确的教育所关心的是个体的自由,唯有这种自由才能带来与个体、与人类整体、与多数人的真正合作;但这种自由并不是通过追求自我的膨胀和成功而获得的。自由伴随着自知而来,当心灵超越和凌驾于因渴望自身安全而制造出来的各种障碍时,自由就会出现。

教育的职责是帮助每个人去发现所有这些心理上的障碍,而不是仅仅把新的行为模式和思维方式强加在他身上。这些强迫永远无法唤醒智慧和创造性的了解,而只会加深个体的局限。无疑,这就是全世界正在发生的事,而这就是我们的问题会层出不穷、与日俱增的原因。

只有当我们开始了解人类生活的深刻意义时,才会有真正的教育;然而要了解它,心灵必须明智地把它自己从想要回报的渴望中——这种渴望滋生了恐惧和遵从——解脱出来。如果我们把孩子视为个人的财产;如果对我们来说,孩子是我们卑微自我的延续和野心的实现,那么我们就会建立起一种没有爱而只追求自我中心利益的环境与社会结构。

The right kind of education is concerned with individual freedom, alone can bring true cooperation with the whole, with the many; freedom is not achieved through the pursuit of one's own aggrandizement and success. Freedom comes with self-knowledge, when the mind goes above and beyond the hindrances it has created for itself through craving its own security.

It is the function of education to help each individual to discover all these psychological hindrances, and not merely impose upon him new patterns of conduct, new modes of thought. Such impositions will never awaken intelligence, creative understanding, but will only further condition the individual. Surely, this is what is happening throughout the world, and that is why our problems continue and multiply.

It is only when we begin to understand the deep significance of human life that there can be true education; but to understand, the mind must intelligently free itself from the desire for reward which breeds fear and conformity. If we regard our children as personal property, if to us they are the continuance of our petty selves and the fulfilment of our ambitions, then we shall build an environment, a social structure in which there is no love, but only the pursuit of self-centred advantages.

一所世俗意义上成功的学校，从作为教育中心的角度来讲多半是失败的。一个巨大而蓬勃的教育机构，成百上千个孩子在其中一起接受教育，还有各种随之而来的炫耀与成功——这样的学校可以生产出银行职员、超级销售员、企业家、政治委员以及技术熟练的肤浅之人；然而，希望只存在于完整的个体身上，而唯有小型的学校才有助于培养出这种人。因此，去建造一些拥有正确的教育者和数量有限的男女学生的学校，远远要比在大型学校里去实施各种最新、最好的教育方法来得更重要。

不幸的是，我们身上最令人困惑的难题之一，就是我们认为一切都必须声势浩大才行。我们大部分人都想要大型的学校，里面尽是一幢幢威风的大楼——即使它们显然并不是正确的教育中心，因为我们想要改变或影响我们的所谓"大多数人"。

但谁是"大多数人"呢？"大多数人"就是你和我。让我们不要迷失在这种想法中，认为"大多数人"必须同样获得正确的教育。考虑"大多数人"就是一种逃避立即行动的方式。如果我们从最近的地方开始，如果我们在自己和孩子的关系中，在自己和朋友以及邻居的关系中觉察自己，那么正确的教育便会普及开来。我们在自己的生活圈子里，以及我们家庭和朋友圈子里的行动，将会产生不断扩大的影响和效果。

A school which is successful in the worldly sense is more often than not a failure as an educational centre. A large and flourishing institution in which hundreds of children are educated together, with all its accompanying show and success, can turn out bank clerks and super-salesmen, industrialists or commissars, superficial people who are technically efficient; but there is hope only in the integrated individual, which only small schools can help to bring about. That is why it is far more important to have schools with a limited number of boys and girls and the right kind of educators, than to practise the latest and best methods in large institutions.

Unfortunately, one of our confusing difficulties is that we must operate on a huge scale. Most of us want large schools with imposing buildings, even though they are obviously not the right kind of educational centres, because we want to transform or affect what we call the masses.

But who are the masses? You and I. Let us not get lost in the thought that the masses must also be rightly educated. The consideration of the mass is a form of escape from immediate action. Right education will become universal if we begin with the immediate, if we are aware of ourselves in our relationship with our children, with our friends and neighbours. Our own action in the world we live in, in the world of our family and friends, will have expanding influence and effect.

通过在我们所有的关系中充分觉察自己，我们会开始发现那些我们现在还不知道的内心的混乱与局限；而在觉察它们的过程中，我们就能了解从而消除它们。没有这种觉察，以及它所带来的自我了解，任何教育改革或其他领域的改革都只会带来更深的对立和痛苦。

建造庞大的教育机构并且雇用一些老师——这些老师依赖于某种教育体系，而没有在他们和每个学生的关系中保持警觉和观察——在这个过程中，我们只是在鼓励积累事实数据、培养能力，以及依照某种模式去机械思考的习惯；但毫无疑问，这一切都无法帮助学生成长为一个完整的人。教育体系，当它掌握在警觉和有想法的教育者手中时，也许会有一点有限的用处，但它无法使人拥有智慧。然而奇怪的是，像"体系""机构"这些词，对我们来说已经变得非常重要。符号已经取代了现实，而我们对此心满意足，觉得它就应该如此；因为现实会令人不安，而幻影却可以带来安慰。

By being fully aware of ourselves in all our relationships we to discover those confusions and limitations within us of which we are now ignorant; and in being aware of them, we shall understand and so dissolve them. Without this awareness and the self-knowledge which it brings, any reform in education or in other fields will only lead to further antagonism and misery.

In building enormous institutions and employing teachers who on a system instead of being alert and observant in their the individual student, we merely encourage the accumulation of facts, the development of capacity, and the habit of thinking mechanically, according to a pattern; but certainly none of this helps the student to grow into an integrated human being. Systems may have a limited use in the hands of alert and thoughtful educators, but they do not make for intelligence. strange that words like"system, ""institution, "have become very important to us. Symbols have taken the place of reality, and we are content that it should be so; for reality is disturbing, while shadows give comfort.

通过大规模的集体教学，无法培育出任何根本性的价值，只有通过仔细研究和了解每一个孩子的困难、倾向和能力才可以；而那些意识到这一点并且真诚渴望去了解他们自己然后帮助年轻人的人，就应该聚集起来，然后建立一所学校，通过帮助孩子变得完整和富有智慧，这所学校将会在孩子的生命中具有极其重大的意义。要开设这样一所学校，并不用一直等到有了必要的资源资金以后才去做。我们可以在家里就成为一个真正的老师，而机遇将会眷顾那些认真的人。

那些爱自己的孩子和他们周围孩子的人，那些因为爱而变得认真的人，他们会设法在某个角落或者自己家里开设一所正确的学校。然后钱就自然会来了——钱是最后考虑的东西。要维持一所施行正确教育的小学校毫无疑问会遭遇财务上的困难，而小学校只有建立在自我奉献而不是一大笔银行存款之上，才会繁荣起来。除非有了爱和了解，否则金钱总是会导致腐败。但如果它真的是一所有价值的学校，你就会找到必要的援助。当有了对孩子的爱，一切都是可能的。

Nothing of fundamental value can be accomplished through mass instruction, but only through the careful study and understanding of the difficulties, tendencies and capacities of each child; and those who are aware of this, and who earnestly desire to understand themselves and help the young, should come together and start a school that will have vital significance in the child's life by helping him to be integrated and intelligent. To start such a school, they need not wait until they have the necessary means. One can be a true teacher at home, and opportunities will come to the earnest.

Those who love their own children and the children about them, and who are therefore in earnest, will see to it that a right school is started somewhere around the corner, or in their own home. Then the money will come — it is the least important consideration. To maintain a small school of the right kind is of course financially difficult; it can flourish only on self-sacrifice, not on a fat bank account. Money invariably corrupts unless there is love and understanding. But if it is really a worthwhile school, the necessary help will be found. When there is love of the child, all things are possible.

只要人们最关心的还是教育机构，孩子便会被忽视。正确的教育者关心的是个人，而不是他有多少学生；这样的教育者将会发现，他可以去开设一所充满活力且意义深远的学校，而一些父母将会支持这样的学校。但老师必须怀有热情，如果他没有兴致，那么他的这所学校就和其他的学校没什么两样了。

如果父母真的爱他们的孩子，他们就会制订法律和采用其他手段来建立配备有正确教育者的小型学校；并且他们不会因为小学校高昂的运营成本和很难找到正确的教育者这些现实问题而打退堂鼓。

然而，他们也应当意识到，他们将不可避免地遭到来自特权阶级、政府以及组织化的宗教的反对，因为这样的学校必然是深具革命性的。真正的革命并不是那种暴力的革命，它是通过培育人类的完整和智慧而来的，这些人通过他们自己的生活，就可以逐渐带来社会的根本性转变。

As long as the institution is the most important consideration, is not. The right kind of educator is concerned with the individual, and not with the number of pupils he has; and such an educator will discover that he can have a vital and significant school which some parents will support. But the teacher must have the flame of interest; if he is lukewarm, he will have an institution like any other.

If parents really love their children, they will employ legislation and other means to establish small schools staffed with the right kind of educators; and they will not be deterred by the fact that small schools are expensive and the right kind of educators difficult to find.

They should realize, however, that there will inevitably be from vested interests, from governments and organized religions, such schools are bound to be deeply revolutionary. True the violent sort; it comes about through cultivating the intelligence of human beings who, by their very life, will gradually create radical changes in society.

然而，最重要的是学校里所有这样的老师都应该自发地聚在一起，而不是通过别人的劝说或者被挑选出来，因为自愿地脱离世俗事物才是一个真正的教育中心唯一正确的基础。如果老师想要帮助彼此，也帮助学生了解正确的价值，他们就必须在日常关系中保持持续而敏锐的觉察。

在一个与世隔绝的小学校里，我们很容易忘记还有一个外面的世界，那个世界有着不断增长的冲突、毁灭和痛苦。那个世界和我们并不是分离的。相反，它就是我们的一部分，因为是我们把它变成了现在的样子。所以，如果想要社会结构发生根本的改变，正确的教育就是第一步。

只有正确的教育才能永久地解决我们的问题与痛苦，而不是各种意识形态、领袖和经济革命；而看到这个事实的真相并非理智或感情上的说服，也不是狡猾的论证。

如果在一所施行正确教育的学校里，它所有教职员工中的核心层是具有奉献精神和充满活力的，它就会吸引其他有着同样志向的人聚集到它这里，而那些不感兴趣的人不久就会发现自己不适合那里了。如果核心层是目标明确和警觉的，那么外围那些冷淡的人就会感到羞愧并且离开了；但如果核心层是漠不关心的态度，那么整个团队就会不稳定和缺乏生气。

But it is of the utmost importance that all the teachers in a school of this kind should come together voluntarily, without being persuaded or chosen; for voluntary freedom from worldliness is the only right foundation for a true educational centre. If the teachers are to help one another and the students to understand right values, there must be constant and alert awareness in their daily relationship.

In the seclusion of a small school one is apt to forget that there is an outside world, with its ever-increasing conflict, destruction and misery. That world is not separate from us. On the contrary, it is part of us, for we have made it what it is; and that is why, if there is to be a fundamental alteration in the structure of society, right education is the first step.

Only right education, and not ideologies, leaders and economic revolutions, can provide a lasting solution for our problems and miseries; and to see the truth of this fact is not a matter of intellectual or emotional persuasion, nor of cunning argument.

If the nucleus of the staff in a school of the right kind is dedicated and vital, it will gather to itself others of the same purpose, and those who are not interested will soon find themselves out of place. If the centre is purposive and alert, the indifferent periphery will wither and drop away; but if the centre is indifferent, then the whole group will be uncertain and weak.

核心层不能只由校长组成。依赖于某个人而存在的热情或兴趣必然会衰退和消亡。这种兴趣是表面的、轻浮的、毫无价值的,因为它可以被转移,然后屈从于另一个人的心血来潮与幻想。如果校长支配着一切,那么显然就不可能会有自由与合作的精神了。一个强势的人物也许能建立一所一流的学校,然而恐惧和奉承也会悄然进入,而通常发生的情况就是,其他员工就变得无足轻重了。

　　这样的团队无益于个体的自由和了解。员工不应该处于校长的支配下,而校长也不应该承担起所有的责任;相反,每个老师都应该感到自己需要对整个学校负责。如果感兴趣的人没几个,那么其他人的冷漠或反对就会阻碍大家的努力或者让努力白费。

The centre cannot be made up of the headmaster alone. interest that depends on one person is sure to wane and die. Such interest is superficial, flighty and worthless, for it can be diverted and made subservient to the whims and fancies of another. If the headmaster is dominating, then the spirit of freedom and cooperation obviously cannot exist. A strong character may build a first-rate school, but fear and subservience creep in, and then it generally happens that the rest of the staff is composed of non-entities.

Such a group is not conducive to individual freedom and understanding. The staff should not be under the domination of the headmaster, and the headmaster should not assume all the responsibility; on the contrary, each teacher should feel responsible for the whole. If there are only a few who are interested, then the indifference or opposition of the rest will impede or stultify the general effort.

我们也许会怀疑，没有一个核心权威，一所学校能否运作？但对于这个问题，我们其实也不知道答案，因为我们从未尝试过它。毫无疑问，在一群真正的教育者中，权威的问题永远不会出现。当所有人都努力变得自由和智慧时，人与人之间各个层面上的合作就有可能了。对那些还没有深刻而持久地投身于正确的教育这项任务的人而言，缺少一个核心权威似乎是一种不切实际的理论；然而如果一个人完全献身于正确的教育，他就不需要别人来督促、指挥或控制了。智慧的老师在施展他们能力的过程中是很灵活的，因为他们在努力达到个体的自由，所以他们会遵守规则，然后去做一些有利于整个学校的必要的工作。认真的兴趣是能力的开始，兴趣和能力都会在实践中得到加强。

One may doubt that a school can be run without a central authority; but one really does not know, because it has never been tried. Surely, in a group of true educators, this problem of authority will never arise. When all are endeavouring to be free and intelligent, cooperation with one another is possible at all levels. To those who have not given themselves over deeply and lastingly to the task of right education, the lack of a central authority may appear to be an impractical theory; but if one is completely dedicated to right education, then one does not require to be urged, directed or controlled. Intelligent teachers are pliable in the exercise of their capacities; attempting to be individually free, they abide by the regulations and do what is necessary for the benefit of the whole school. Serious interest is the beginning of capacity, and both are strengthened by application.

如果一个人不了解服从在心理上暗含的意义，那么仅仅决定不去跟从权威将只会导致混乱。这种混乱的产生并不是由于缺少权威，而是因为缺乏对正确教育深刻的、共同的兴趣。如果有了真正的兴趣，每个老师这边都会进行持续不断和深思熟虑的调整，来满足运作一所学校的种种需要和必需品。任何一种关系中都不可避免地会有摩擦和误解，然而如果没有了由共同兴趣所带来的紧密感情，这些摩擦和误解就会被放大。

在一所施行正确教育的学校里，所有老师之间必须要有不受限制的合作。全体教员应该经常碰头，详细讨论学校的各种问题，当他们就某种做法达成一致以后，很显然执行这种已经决定下来的东西就不会遇到阻碍了。如果多数人采纳的某个决定不能获得某个老师的认可，可以把它放到下次教员会议上再进行讨论。

If one does not understand the psychological implications of obedience, merely to decide not to follow authority will only lead to confusion. Such confusion is not due to the absence of authority, but to the lack of deep and mutual interest in right education. If there is real interest, there is constant and thoughtful adjustment on the part of every teacher to the demands and necessities of running a school. In any relationship, frictions and misunderstandings are inevitable; but they become exaggerated when there is not the binding affection of common interest.

There must be unstinted cooperation among all the teachers in a school of the right kind. The whole staff should meet often, to talk over the various problems of the school; and when they have agreed upon a certain course of action, there should obviously be no difficulty in carrying out what has been decided. If some decision taken by the majority does not meet with the approval of a particular teacher, it can be discussed again at the next meeting of the faculty.

任何老师都不应该惧怕校长，而校长也不应该对那些年纪大的老师心存畏惧。只有当感觉到所有人都是完全平等时，才可能达成愉快的共识。让一所施行正确教育的学校中充盈着这种平等感是很重要的，因为只有当优越感和它的反面都不复存在时，才会有真正的合作。如果有了彼此间的信任，任何困难或误解都不会只是被束之高阁，我们将会去面对它，然后信任就会恢复。

如果教师不能确信自己的天职和兴趣，他们之间就必然会有妒忌和敌对，他们会把自己所拥有的一切能量都消耗在琐碎的细节以及浪费时间和精力的争吵上；反之，如果有了那种想要带来正确教育的强烈兴趣，生气和表面的分歧就会很快过去。然后那些被过度夸大的细节就会呈现出它们正常的比重，摩擦与个人的敌意将被我们视为徒劳无益的和破坏性的，所有的对话与讨论都会帮助我们去发现"什么才是对的"，而不是"谁才是对的"。

No teacher should be afraid of the headmaster, nor should the headmaster feel intimidated by the older teachers. Happy agreement is possible only when there is a feeling of absolute equality among all. It is essential that this feeling of equality prevail in the right kind of school, for there can be real cooperation only when the sense of superiority and its opposite are non- existent. If there is mutual trust, any difficulty or misunderstanding will not just be brushed aside, but will be faced, and confidence restored.

If the teachers are not sure of their own vocation and is bound to be envy and antagonism among them, and they will whatever energies they have over trifling details and wasteful whereas, irritations and superficial disagreements will quickly be passed over if there is a burning interest in bringing about the right kind of education. Then the details which loom so large assume their normal proportions, friction and personal antagonisms are seen to be vain and destructive, and all talks and discussions help one to find out what is right and not who is right.

为了一个共同的目标而在一起工作的人,应该时常讨论各种困难和误解,因为这可以帮助澄清也许存在于我们自身思维中的任何混乱。当有了目的一致的兴趣,老师之间同样也会有坦诚和友谊,他们之间永远不会产生敌意;可是如果没有了兴趣,那么尽管表面上他们也许会为了彼此的利益而合作,但总是会存在着冲突和敌意。

当然了,也许还有一些其他的因素会导致团体成员间的摩擦。某个老师也许劳累过度,另一个也许有一些个人或家庭的烦恼,还有一些人或许对他们在做的事并没有很大的兴趣。显然,所有这些问题都可以在教师会议上研究解决,因为共同的兴趣可以促成合作。很显然,如果少数人包揽了一切,而其他人袖手旁观,就不可能创造出充满活力的事物。

Difficulties and misunderstandings should always be talked over by those who are working together with a common intention, for it helps to clarify any confusion that may exist in one's own thinking. When there is purposive interest, there is also frankness and comradeship among the teachers, and antagonism can never arise between them; but if that interest is lacking, though superficially they may cooperate for their mutual advantage, there will always be conflict and enmity.

There may be, of course, other factors that are causing friction among the members of the staff. One teacher may be overworked, another may have personal or family worries, and perhaps still others do not feel deeply interested in what they are doing. Surely, all these problems can be thrashed out at the teachers' meeting, for mutual interest makes for cooperation. It is obvious that nothing vital can be created if a few do everything and the rest sit back.

工作的平等分配可以让所有人都有空闲时间，很显然，每个人都必须要有一定的闲暇。一个劳累过度的老师，对他自己和其他人而言，都会成为一个问题。如果一个人的压力过重，他容易变得缺乏生气和懒惰——特别是当他在做着自己不喜欢的事情时。如果身体或脑子不停地工作，就不可能恢复元气；而关于空闲时间的问题，可以用一种大家都能接受的友好方式去解决。

每个人闲暇时光的构成也是不同的。对于某些对自己的工作有着极大兴趣的人来说，工作本身就是一种闲暇；做自己感兴趣的事——比如做研究——这本身就是一种放松。而对另一些人来说，闲暇或许是躲到与世隔绝的地方去。

如果教育者想要有一些自己的时间，他就必须只负责他能轻松应对的、适当数量的学生。当老师被一大群管不过来的学生压得喘不过气时，师生之间就几乎不可能会有直接和充满活力的关系了。

保持学校的小型化还有另一个原因。限制班级学生人数很显然是非常重要的，这样教育者就可以充分注意到每一个学生。当学生太多时，他就很难做到这点了，于是，惩罚和奖励就成了一种强制执行纪律的简便方法。

Equal distribution of work gives leisure to all, and each one must obviously have a certain amount of leisure. An overworked teacher becomes a problem to himself and to others. If one is under too great a strain, one is apt to become lethargic, indolent, and especially so if one is doing something which is not to one's liking. Recuperation is not possible if there is constant activity, physical or mental; but this question of leisure can be settled in a friendly manner acceptable to all.

What constitutes leisure differs with each individual. To some greatly interested in their work, that work itself is leisure; the very action of interest, such as study, is a form of relaxation. To others, leisure may be a withdrawal into seclusion.

If the educator is to have a certain amount of time to himself, he must be responsible only for the number of students that he can easily cope with. A direct and vital relationship between teacher and student is almost impossible when the teacher is weighed down by large and unmanageable numbers.

This is still another reason why schools should be kept small. It is obviously important to have a very limited number of students in a class, so that the educator can give his full attention to each one. When the group is too large he cannot do this, and then punishment and reward become a convenient way of enforcing discipline.

正确的教育不可能一大群人同时进行。研究每个孩子需要耐心、警觉和智慧。观察孩子的兴趣、才能、性情，了解他的困难之处，考虑到他的遗传和父母的影响，而不是仅仅把他加以归类——这一切都需要一颗敏捷和柔韧的心，不受任何体系或偏见的束缚。它需要技巧和强烈的兴趣，最重要的还是要有关爱之情；而培养具备这些品质的教育者是我们当前的主要难题之一。

智慧以及个体自由的精神，应该始终弥漫在整个学校里。这一点绝不能疏忽，偶尔随便地提一下"自由"和"智慧"这些字眼，是没多大意义的。

学生和老师应定期碰面，然后讨论与整个团体利益相关的所有事宜，这一点尤为重要。应当成立一个学生会，老师的声音也能在其中得以呈现，学生会负责商讨解决关于纪律、卫生、食物等所有问题，它同样可以帮助去引导那些有点任性、冷漠或顽固的学生。

The right kind of education is not possible en masse. To child requires patience, alertness and intelligence. To observe the child's tendencies, his aptitudes, his temperament, to understand his difficulties, to take into account his heredity and parental influence and not merely regard him as belonging to a certain category — all this calls for a swift and pliable mind, untrammelled by any system or prejudice. It calls intense interest and, above all, a sense of affection; and to produce educators endowed with these qualities is one of our major problems today.

The spirit of individual freedom and intelligence should pervade the whole school at all times. This can hardly be left to chance, and the casual mention at odd moments of the words "freedom" and "intelligence" has very little significance.

It is particularly important that students and teachers meet discuss all matters relating to the well-being of the whole group. A student council should be formed, on which the teachers are represented, which can thrash out all the problems of discipline, cleanliness, food and so on, and which can also help to guide any students who may be somewhat self-indulgent, indifferent or obstinate.

学生应该从他们身边选举出负责执行决策、帮助进行常规监管的同学。毕竟，学校里的自我管理是为今后生活中的自我管理做准备的。如果孩子在学校的时候学会了在任何与他日常生活问题相关的讨论中去体谅他人、保持客观和智慧，那么当他长大以后，他就能有效而冷静地去面对生活中更大、更复杂的考验。学校应当鼓励孩子去理解彼此的困难、独特性、情绪和脾气，因为这样的话，当他们长大以后，他们就会对其他人更加体贴和耐心。

同样的自由精神和智慧也应该明确地体现在孩子的学习中。要孩子变得具有创造性，而不仅仅是一个机器人，就不应该鼓励学生接受各种公式和结论。即使在科学研究中，我们也应该和他一起去推理论证，帮助他看清问题的全貌，然后让他自己去作出判断。

The students should choose from among themselves those who are to be responsible for the carrying out of decisions and for helping with the general supervision. After all, self-government in the school is a preparation for self-government in later life. If, while he is at school, the child learns to be considerate, impersonal and intelligent in any discussion pertaining to his daily problems, when he is older he will be able to meet effectively and dispassionately the greater and more complex trials of life. The school should encourage the children to understand one another's difficulties and peculiarities, moods and tempers; for then, as they grow up, they will be more thoughtful and patient in their relationship with others.

This same spirit of freedom and intelligence should be evident also in the child's studies. If he is to be creative and not merely an automaton, the student should not be encouraged to accept formulas and conclusions. Even in the study of a science, one should reason with him, helping him to see the problem in its entirety and to use his own judgment.

那么如何处理"指导"的问题？难道就不需要任何"指导"了吗？这个问题的答案取决于"指导"是什么意思。如果老师已经抛弃了内心所有的恐惧和想要支配的欲望，他们就可以帮助学生走向创造性的了解和自由；但如果老师有意或无意地想要指引学生朝着某个特定目标前进，很显然他们就妨碍了学生的成长。指导学生朝向某个目标——不管这个目标是学生自己制订的，还是别人强加的——都损害了创造性。

如果教育者关心的是个体的自由，而不是他自己的偏见，他就会鼓励孩子去了解他自己周围的环境、他的性格、他的宗教和家庭背景，以及这些东西可能会在他身上产生的所有影响和效果，通过这种方式，他就能帮助孩子发现那份自由。如果老师自己内心有了爱与自由，他们就会很用心地去处理每一个学生的需求和困难；因此，他们不会成为仅仅只是根据方法和公式来运作的机器人，而是永远保持警觉和留心的自发的人。

But what about guidance? Should there be no guidance whatsoever? The answer to this question depends on what is meant by "guidance. "If in their hearts the teachers have put away all fear and all desire for domination, then they can help the student towards creative understanding and freedom; but if there is a conscious or unconscious desire to guide him towards a particular goal, then obviously they are hindering his development. Guidance towards a particular objective, whether created by oneself or imposed by another, impairs creativeness.

If the educator is concerned with the freedom of the individual, and not with his own preconceptions, he will help the child to discover that freedom by encouraging him to understand his own environment, his own temperament, his religious and family background, with all the influences and effects they can possibly have on him. If there is love and freedom in the hearts of the teachers themselves, they will approach each student mindful of his needs and difficulties; and then they will not be mere automatons, operating according to methods and formulas, but spontaneous human beings, ever alert and watchful.

正确的教育同样应该帮助学生去发现他最感兴趣的是什么。如果学生没有找到自己真正的天职,他的一生似乎就虚度了,当他做的是一些自己不想做的事情时,他会感到沮丧。如果本想成为艺术家的他,却做了办公室的职员,那他的一生都会抱怨不断,并且日益憔悴下去。所以重要的是每个人都要找到他想做的事,并且看看这件事是否值得做。男孩子也许会想要成为一名军人,但在他参军之前,我们应该帮助他去发现军人的职业是否对全人类有益。

正确的教育不仅要帮助学生发展他的能力,更要帮助他了解他自己最大的兴趣。在一个被战争、毁灭和痛苦撕裂的世界里,我们必须能够建立起一种全新的社会秩序,并且带来一种截然不同的生活方式。

建立一个和平、文明社会的责任主要就落在教育者身上,而很显然——请不要为这种说法而情绪激动——他有很大的机会可以为实现这种社会变革效力。正确的教育并不依赖于任何政府的法规,或者任何特定体系的方法;它掌握在我们自己手中,掌握在父母和老师的手中。

The right kind of education should also help the student to discover what he is most interested in. If he does not find his true vocation, all his life will seem wasted; he will feel frustrated doing something which he does not want to do. If he wants to be an artist and instead becomes a clerk in some office, he will spend his life grumbling and pining away. So it is important for each one to find out what he wants to do, and then to see if it is worth doing. A boy may want to be a soldier; but before he takes up soldiering, he should be helped to discover whether the military vocation is beneficial to the whole of mankind.

Right education should help the student, not only to develop his capacities, but to understand his own highest interest. In a world wars, destruction and misery, one must be able to build a new social order and bring about a different way of living.

The responsibility for building a peaceful and enlightened chiefly with the educator, and it is obvious, without becoming emotionally stirred up about it, that he has a very great opportunity to help in achieving that social transformation. The right kind of education does not depend on the regulations of any government or the methods of any particular system; it lies in our own hands, in the hands of the parents and the teachers.

如果父母真的关心他们的孩子,他们将会建立一个新的社会;但从根本上来讲,大多数父母并不关心孩子,所以他们抽不出时间来处理这个最为紧迫的问题。他们有时间赚钱、有时间娱乐、有时间进行各种仪式和崇拜,却没有时间来考虑一下,对他们的孩子而言,什么才是正确的教育?这是一个大多数人都不愿去面对的事实。因为面对它意味着必须要放弃自己的娱乐和种种消遣,他们当然不愿意这么做了。于是,他们把自己的孩子送去学校,而那里的老师也并不比他们更关心这些孩子。为什么老师要去关心?教书对他来说只是一份工作、一种谋生手段而已。

如果我们看到帘幕背后的事物,就会发现我们所建立的这个世界是多么的肤浅、虚伪和丑陋,而我们却在装饰着帘幕,希望一切都会莫名其妙地好起来。不幸的是,大多数人除了赚钱、获取权力、追求性快感以外,也许对生活并不是很热忱。他们并不想去面对生活中其他的复杂问题,所以,当他们的孩子长大以后,他们也会和自己的父母一样不成熟和不完整,不断地与自己以及这个世界斗争。

If parents really cared for their children, they would build a new society; but fundamentally most parents do not care, and so they have no time for this most urgent problem. They have time for making money, for amusements, for rituals and worship, but no time to consider what is the right kind of education for their children. This is a fact that the majority of people do not want to face. To face it might mean that they would have to give up their amusements and distractions, and certainly they are not willing to do that. So they send their children off to schools where the teacher cares no more for them than they do. Why should he care? Teaching is merely a job to him, a way of earning money.

The world we have created is so superficial, so artificial, so looks behind the curtain; and we decorate the curtain, hoping that everything will somehow come right. Most people are unfortunately not very earnest about life except, perhaps, when it comes to making money, gaining power, or pursuing sexual excitement. They do not want to face the other complexities of life, and that is why, when their children grow up, they are as immature and unintegrated as their parents, constantly battling with themselves and with the world.

我们如此轻易地说"我们爱自己的孩子",然而当我们接受了现有的社会环境,当我们不想从根本上转变这个毁灭性的社会时,我们的心中还有爱吗?只要我们还是指望专家来教育我们的孩子,混乱和不幸就会延续下去;因为专家关心的是部分而非整体,他们自己就是不完整的。

如今,教育者并没有成为无比光荣和责任重大的职业,而是受到了轻视,大部分教育者都固守于例行公事。他们并没有真正地去关心完整和智慧,而只关心知识信息的给予;一个眼看着他周围的世界正在崩塌,却只是去给予知识信息的人,不算是一个教育者。

教育者不仅仅是知识信息的给予者,也是指明通往智慧和真理之路的人。真理远比老师更重要。寻找真理就是宗教。真理不分国界,也无关教义,你无法在任何寺庙或教堂里找到它。没有对真理的寻找,社会很快就会衰退。要创造一个崭新的社会,我们每个人都必须成为真正的老师,这意味着我们必须既是学生也是老师,我们必须进行自我教育。

We say so easily that we love our children; but is there love in our hearts when we accept the existing social conditions, when we do not want to bring about a fundamental transformation in this destructive society? And as long as we look to the specialists to educate our children, this confusion and misery will continue; for the specialists, being concerned with the part and not with the whole, are themselves unintegrated.

Instead of being the most honoured and responsible occupation, education is now considered slightingly, and most educators are fixed in a routine. They are not really concerned with integration and intelligence, but with the imparting of information; and a man who merely imparts information with the world crashing about him is not an educator.

An educator is not merely a giver of information; he is one who points the way to wisdom, to truth. Truth is far more important than the teacher. The search for truth is religion, and truth is of no country, of no creed, it is not to be found in any temple or church. Without the search for truth, society soon decays. To create a new society, each one of us has to be a true teacher, which means that we have to be both the pupil and the master; we have to educate ourselves.

要建立一种新的社会秩序,那么仅仅为了赚取一份薪水而教书的人,很显然是没资格成为老师的。把教育当成一种谋生手段,就是在为了一己私利而剥削孩子。在一个开明的社会里,老师无须担心自己的福利问题,社会将供给他生活所需。

真正的老师不是那个建立起令人惊叹的教育机构的人,也不是政客手中的工具,更不是那个受缚于理想、信仰或国家的人。真正的老师内在富有,因此他不为自己谋求任何东西;他没有野心,也不寻求任何形式的权力;他不会把教书作为一种获取地位或权威的手段,因而他摆脱了社会的强制和政府的控制。这样的老师对于进步的文明来说是至关重要的,因为真正的文明不是建立在工程师和技术人员之上,而是建立在教育者之上。

If a new social order is to be established, those who teach merely to earn a salary can obviously have no place as teachers. To regard education as a means of livelihood is to exploit the children for one's own advantage. In an enlightened society, teachers will have no concern for their own welfare, and the community will provide for their needs.

The true teacher is not he who has built up an impressive educational organization, nor he who is an instrument of the politicians, nor he who is bound to an ideal, a belief or a country. The true teacher is inwardly rich and therefore asks nothing for himself; he is not ambitious and seeks no power in any form; he does not use teaching as a means of acquiring position or authority, and therefore he is free from the compulsion of society and the control of governments. Such teachers have the primary place in an enlightened civilization, for true culture is founded, not on the engineers and technicians, but on the educators.

第六章

父母和老师

CHAPTER VI
PARENTS AND TEACHERS

正确的教育从教育者开始，教育者必须了解他自己，并且脱离既定的思维模式，因为他是什么，他传授的就是什么。如果他没有接受过正确的教育，那么除了那些他所接受的同样机械化的知识之外，他还能教给别人什么呢？因此，问题不在孩子，而在父母和老师；问题在于要去教育那个教育者。

如果我们作为教育者不了解我们自己，如果我们不了解我们和孩子的关系，而只是将各种知识信息塞给他，从而使他通过考试，我们又怎么可能带来一种新的教育呢？学生需要引导和帮助，但如果那个指导者、那个帮助者自己都是混乱的、狭隘的、受理论支配的，那么他的学生自然也会和他一样，于是教育就变成了助长混乱和斗争的源头。

如果我们看到了这个真相，我们就会意识到着手对自己进行正确的教育是多么重要。关心我们自身的"再教育"，远比担忧孩子未来的幸福和安全更加必要。

The right kind of education begins with the educator, who must understand himself and be free from established patterns of what he is, that he imparts. If he has not been rightly educated, what can he teach except the same mechanical knowledge on which he himself has been brought up? The problem, therefore, is not the child, but the parent and the teacher; the problem is to educate the educator.

If we who are the educators do not understand ourselves, if not understand our relationship with the child but merely stuff information and make him pass examinations, how can we about a new kind of education? The pupil is there to be guided and helped; but if the guide, the helper is himself confusednarrow and theory-ridden, then naturally his pupil will be what he is, and education becomes a source of further confusion and strife.

If we see the truth of this, we will realize how important it is that we begin to educate ourselves rightly. To be concerned with our own re-education is far more necessary than to worry about the future well-being and security of the child.

对教育者进行教育——也就是让他了解自己——是最艰难的任务之一,因为我们大多数人都已经固守于某种思想体系或行动模式;我们沉迷于某种意识形态、宗教或特定的行为准则,所以我们才教导孩子"思考什么",而不是教他"如何思考"。

此外,父母和老师的内心基本上被自己的冲突和悲伤占据。不管富有还是贫穷,大多数父母都沉浸在他们个人的忧虑和苦恼中。他们并没有深切关注当今社会的退化和道德的堕落,而只是想让自己的孩子全副武装地上阵,然后在社会上出人头地。他们担忧自己孩子的未来,于是急着让他们接受教育,确保他以后能有个安稳的职位,或者能找个好人家结婚。

与人们通常所认为的恰恰相反,大多数父母其实并不爱他们的孩子——虽然他们嘴上说爱。如果父母真的爱自己的孩子,就不会强调与人类整体相对立的家庭和国家——这种强调制造出了人与人之间的社会和种族区分,由此带来了战争与饥饿。令人无比惊奇的是,在人们需要接受严格培训才能成为律师或医生的同时,他们却可以不经过任何培训就成为父母,去担任这项最为重要的任务。

To educate the educator — that is, to have him understand himself — is one of the most difficult undertakings, because most of us are already crystallized within a system of thought or a pattern of action; we have already given ourselves over to some ideology, to a religion, or to a particular standard of conduct. That is why we teach the child what to think and not how to think.

Moreover, parents and teachers are largely occupied with their own conflicts and sorrows. Rich or poor, most parents are absorbed in their personal worries and trials. They are not gravely concerned about the present social and moral deterioration, but only desire that their children shall be equipped to get on in the world. They are anxious about the future of their children, eager to have them educated to hold secure positions, or to marry well.

Contrary to what is generally believed, most parents do not love their children, though they talk of loving them. If parents really loved their children, there would be no emphasis laid on the family and the nation as opposed to the whole, which creates social and racial divisions between men and brings about war and starvation. It is really extraordinary that, while people are rigorously trained to be lawyers or doctors, they may become parents without undergoing any training whatsoever to fit them for this all-important task.

通常来讲，家庭带有隔离排外的倾向，它助长了普遍化的孤立过程，从而变成了导致社会衰退的因素。只有存在爱和了解，孤立隔绝的围墙才会被推倒，那时家庭就不再是一个封闭的圈子，它既不会成为监狱，也不会成为避难所；那时父母不仅能够与自己的孩子交流，也能与他们的邻居交流。

无数父母沉浸在自己的各种问题中，然后把为孩子谋求幸福的责任转嫁给了老师；所以重要的是，教育者同样也要帮忙去教育父母。

教育者必须和父母谈话，向他们解释这个世界混乱的局面正是他们自身混乱的反映。他必须向他们指出，科学进步本身是无法带来现有价值的彻底改变的；而培养技术——如今它被称为教育——并没有带给人类自由，或者让人类变得更幸福；制约学生，使他接受现有的环境，这无助于智慧。他必须告诉父母他在试图为他们的孩子所做的事情，以及他是如何着手去做的。他必须唤起父母的信心，不是凭着一种专家对待无知外行的权威姿态，而是通过和他们讨论孩子的性格、困难、天资，等等，以这种方式来唤醒他们的信心。

More often than not, the family, with its separate tendencies, encourages the general process of isolation, thereby becoming a deteriorating factor in society. It is only when there is love and understanding that the walls of isolation are broken down, and then the family is no longer a closed circle, it is neither a prison nor a refuge; then the parents are in communion, not only with their children, but also with their neighbours.

Being absorbed in their own problems, many parents shift to the teacher the responsibility for the well-being of their children; and then it is important that the educator help in the education of the parents as well.

He must talk to them, explaining that the confused state of mirrors their own individual confusion. He must point out that progress in itself cannot bring about a radical change in existing values; that technical training, which is now called education, has not given man freedom or made him any happier; and that to condition the student to accept the present environment is not conducive to intelligence. He must what he is attempting to do for their child, and how he is setting about it. He has to awaken the parents' confidence, not by assuming the authority of a specialist dealing with ignorant laymen, but by talking over with them the child's temperament, difficulties, aptitudes and so on.

如果老师能把孩子当成一个个体，对他产生真正的兴趣，父母就会信赖老师。在这个过程中，老师既是在教育父母，也是在教育他自己——而反过来，他也同时在向父母学习。正确的教育是双方共同的任务，它需要耐心、关怀和爱。一个文明社会中的开明的老师，会去研究解决如何培养孩子的问题，一系列由此展开的试验会先由那些有兴趣的老师和关心孩子的父母来小规模地进行。

父母有没有问过自己，为什么要孩子？他们要孩子是为了延续他们的姓氏，为了让孩子来继承他们的财产吗？他们想要孩子仅仅是为了自己的快乐，为了满足自己的情感需求吗？如果是这样，孩子就仅仅成了父母欲望和恐惧的投射。

当父母经由对孩子错误的教育而培养了妒忌、敌意和野心时，他们还能声称爱自己的孩子吗？难道不正是这种"爱"激发了国家和种族的对立吗？这种对立导致了战争、毁灭和彻底的不幸，难道不正是这种"爱"使人类在宗教和意识形态的名义下互相残杀吗？

If the teacher takes a real interest in the child as an individual, the parents will have confidence in him. In this process, the teacher is educating the parents as well as himself, while learning from them in return. Right education is a mutual task demanding patience, consideration and affection. Enlightened teachers in an enlightened community could work out this problem of how to bring up children, and experiments along these lines should be made on a small scale by interested teachers and thoughtful parents.

Do parents ever ask themselves why they have children? Do they have children to perpetuate their name, to carry on their property? Do they want children merely for the sake of their own delight, to satisfy their own emotional needs? If so, then the children become a mere projection of the desires and fears of their parents.

Can parents claim to love their children when, by educating them wrongly, they foster envy, enmity and ambition? Is it love that stimulates the national and racial antagonisms which lead to war, destruction and utter misery, that sets man against man in the name of religions and ideologies?

通过允许孩子甘受错误的教育，也通过他们自己生活中的行为方式，很多父母鼓励了孩子走向冲突和悲伤；而当孩子长大并且遭受痛苦时，他们就为他祈祷，或者为孩子的行为找出各种借口。父母为孩子而痛苦是一种因占有而引起的自怜——只有当没有爱时，才会有这种自怜。

如果父母爱自己的孩子，他们就会去发现怎样与财产保持正确的关系，因为正是占有的本能赋予了财产巨大和错误的意义，而这种巨大和错误的意义正在毁灭这个世界；如果父母爱自己的孩子，他们就会消除嫉妒和争吵，然后着手从根本上去改变当今的社会结构。

只要我们还是想让自己的孩子变得有权有势，拥有更高、更好的地位，或者越来越成功，我们的心中就是没有爱的，因为对成功的崇拜助长了冲突与不幸。爱自己的孩子，就是与他们保持充分的交流，就是设法让他们拥有一种能帮助他们变得敏感、智慧和完整的教育。

Many parents encourage the child in the ways of conflict and sorrow, not only by allowing him to be submitted to the wrong kind of education, but by the manner in which they conduct their own lives; and then, when the child grows up and suffers, they pray for him or find excuses for his behaviour. The suffering of parents for their children is a form of possessive self-pity which exists only when there is no love.

If parents love their children, they will discover what is right relationship to property; for the possessive instinct has given property an enormous and false significance which is destroying the world. If parents love their children, they will do away with envy and strife, and will set about altering fundamentally the structure of present-day society.

As long as we want our children to be powerful, to have bigger and better positions, to become more and more successful, there is no love in our hearts; for the worship of success encourages conflict and misery. To love one's children is to be in complete communion with them; it is to see that they have the kind of education that will help them to be sensitive, intelligent and integrated.

当一个老师决定投身于教育事业时，他首先要问自己的一件事就是，他所认为的教育究竟是什么。他会以惯有的方式去教授通常的科目吗？他是想要制约孩子，使他成为社会机器中的一个齿轮，还是帮助他成为一个完整和具有创造性的人？如果教育者要帮助学生审视和了解周围的种种价值和影响——学生就是这些价值和影响的一部分——教育者是不是自己必须先要觉察到它们？如果一个人双目失明，他还能帮助别人渡到彼岸吗？

毫无疑问，老师自己必须首先开始去观察。他必须时时警觉，敏锐地觉察到自己的思想和感受，觉察他自己受制约的方式，觉察他的各种行动和反应；因为从这种警觉中就会产生智慧，通过这种警觉，他和别人的关系，以及他和事物的关系就会发生彻底的改变。

The first thing a teacher must ask himself, when he decides that he wants to teach, is what exactly he means by teaching. Is he going to teach the usual subjects in the habitual way? Does he want to condition the child to become a cog in the social machine, or help him to be an integrated, creative human being? And if the educator is to help the student to examine and understand the values and influences that surround him and of which he is a part, must he not be aware of them himself? If one is blind, can one help others to cross to the other shore?

Surely, the teacher himself must first begin to see. He must be constantly alert, intensely aware of his own thoughts and feelings, aware of the ways in which he is conditioned, aware of his activities and his responses; for out of this watchfulness comes intelligence, and with it a radical transformation in his relationship to people and to things.

智慧与通过考试无关。智慧是自发的感知，它让人变得坚强和自由。要唤醒孩子内心的智慧，我们必须开始亲自去了解什么是智慧；因为如果我们自己在很多方面仍旧缺乏智慧，又怎能要求孩子变得智慧呢？问题不仅在于学生有困难，我们自己也有困难：日积月累的恐惧、苦恼和挫折——我们一直无法摆脱这些东西。为了帮助孩子变得智慧，我们必须打破内心的种种障碍——正是它们使我们变得迟钝和缺乏思考。

　　如果我们自己仍在追求安全感，又如何教导孩子不去寻求个人的安全感呢？如果我们作为父母和老师，没有对生活保持完全的开放，如果我们在自己周围竖立起自我保护的围墙，那么孩子还会有希望吗？要发现奋力追求安全感的真正意义——正是追求安全感导致了世界如此混乱——我们就必须开始通过觉察我们的心理过程，来唤醒自己的智慧；我们必须开始质疑如今围绕在我们身边的所有价值。

Intelligence has nothing to do with the passing of examinations. Intelligence is the spontaneous perception which makes a man strong and free. To awaken intelligence in a child, we must begin to understand for ourselves what intelligence is; for how can we ask a child to be intelligent if we ourselves remain unintelligent in so many ways? The problem is not only the student's difficulties, but also our own: the cumulative fears, unhappiness and frustrations of which we are not free. In order to help the child to be intelligent, we have to break down within ourselves those hindrances which make us dull and thoughtless.

How can we teach children not to seek personal security if we ourselves are pursuing it? What hope is there for the child if we who are parents and teachers are not entirely vulnerable to life, if we erect protective walls around ourselves? To discover the true significance of this struggle for security, which is causing such chaos in the world, we must begin to awaken our own intelligence by being aware of our psychological processes; we must begin to question all the values which now enclose us.

我们不应该再继续不加考虑地顺应某种模式——某种我们碰巧在其中被培养长大的模式。如果我们不了解自己，又怎么可能会有个人的和谐，以及由此而来的社会和谐呢？除非教育者了解他自己，除非他看到自身局限的反应，并且开始把自己从现有价值中解脱出来，否则他又怎么可能唤醒孩子心中的智慧呢？而如果他无法唤醒孩子的智慧，他的作用又是什么呢？

只有通过了解我们自己思想和感受的方式，我们才能真正帮助孩子成为一个自由的人；如果教育者无比关心这一点，他就会保持敏锐的觉察，不仅觉察孩子，也觉察他自己。

我们中极少有人会去观察自己的思想和感受。如果那些思想和感受很明显是丑陋的，我们便不会去了解它们的全部意义，而只会试图抑制它们，或者把它们推到一边。我们并没有深刻地觉察自己，我们的思想和感受是固定的、习惯性的。我们学习了一些科目，收集起一些信息，然后努力把它传递给孩子。

We should not continue to fit thoughtlessly into the pattern in which we happen to have been brought up. How can there ever be harmony in the individual and so in society if we do not understand ourselves? Unless the educator understands himself, unless he sees his own conditioned responses and is beginning to free himself from existing values, how can he possibly awaken intelligence in the child? And if he cannot awaken intelligence in the child, then what is his function?

It is only by understanding the ways of our own thought and feeling that we can truly help the child to be a free human being; and if the educator is vitally concerned with this, he will be keenly aware, not only of the child, but also of himself.

Very few of us observe our own thoughts and feelings. If obviously ugly, we do not understand their full significance, but merely try to check them or push them aside. We are not deeply aware of ourselves; our thoughts and feelings are stereotyped, automatic. We learn a few subjects, gather some information, and then try to pass it on to the children.

然而,如果我们有强烈的兴趣,就不仅仅会设法寻找世界各地所进行的各种教育试验,也会想要搞清楚我们自己对这整个问题的态度;我们将会自问:我们为什么要教育孩子和自己?这样做的目的是什么?我们会去探究生活的意义,探究个人与社会的关系,等等。毫无疑问,教育者必须要觉察到这些问题,然后努力帮助孩子去发现关于它们的真相,而不是把他们自己的癖好和思维习惯投射到他身上。

仅仅遵循一个体系,无论是政治体系还是教育体系,都永远无法解决我们无数的社会问题。而了解我们处理任何一个问题的方式,远比了解问题本身更加重要。

But if we are vitally interested, we shall not only try to find out what experiments are being made in education in different parts of the world, but we shall want to be very clear about our own approach to this whole question; we shall ask ourselves why and to what purpose we are educating the children and ourselves; we shall inquire into the meaning of existence, into the relationship of the individual to society, and so on. Surely, educators must be aware of these problems and try to help the child to discover the truth concerning them, without projecting upon him their own idiosyncrasies and habits of thought.

Merely to follow a system, whether political or educational, will never solve our many social problems; and it is far more important to understand the manner of our approach to any problem, than to understand the problem itself.

如果想让孩子摆脱恐惧——不管是对他们父母的恐惧，对环境的恐惧，还是对上帝的恐惧——教育者自己必须无所畏惧。但这就是困难所在：我们很难找到一些自身没有成为恐惧的牺牲品的老师。恐惧让我们的思维变得狭隘，并且制约了自发创造精神，一个心存恐惧的老师显然无法传达出无所畏惧的深层含义。就像良善一样，恐惧也具有传染性。如果教育者自己暗地里在害怕，他就会将这种恐惧传染给他的学生，虽然这种传染一时半会儿看不出来。

举个例子，假设一个老师惧怕公众舆论，他发现自己的恐惧很是荒谬，但还是无法越过它。那他要怎么做呢？至少他可以向自己承认这一点，通过讲述他自己心理上的反应，并且开诚布公地和学生来讨论它，他就可以帮助他的学生了解恐惧。这种坦率和真诚的态度将会极大地鼓舞学生，让他们可以对自己、对老师也保持同样的开诚布公和坦率直接。

要给予孩子自由，教育者自己必须意识到自由的内涵和全部意义。任何形式的榜样和强制都无助于带来自由，然而，只有在自由中才会有自我发现和洞见。

If children are to be free from fear — whether of their parents, environment, or of God — the educator himself must have no fear. But that is the difficulty: to find teachers who are not themselves the prey of some kind of fear. Fear narrows down thought and limits initiative, and a teacher who is fearful obviously cannot convey the deep significance of being without fear. Like goodness, fear is contagious. If the educator himself is secretly afraid, he will pass that fear on to his students, although its contamination may not be immediately seen.

Suppose, for example, that a teacher is afraid of public opinion; he sees the absurdity of his fear, and yet cannot go beyond it. What is he to do? He can at least acknowledge it to himself, and can help his students to understand fear by bringing out his own psychological reaction and openly talking it over with them. This honest and sincere approach will greatly encourage the students to be equally open and direct with themselves and with the teacher.

To give freedom to the child, the educator himself must be aware of the implications and the full significance of freedom. Example and compulsion in any form do not help to bring about freedom, and it is only in freedom that there can be self-discovery and insight.

孩子会被他周围的人、事、物影响，正确的教育者应当帮他揭示出这些影响以及它们真正的价值。正确的价值并不是通过社会权威或传统发现的，只有个体的深刻思考才能揭示出它们。

如果深刻地理解了这一点，我们会从一开始就鼓励学生，唤醒他对于当今个体和社会价值的洞察力。我们会鼓励他去寻找，不是寻找一套特定的价值观念，而是寻找所有事物的真正价值。我们会帮助他变得无所畏惧——摆脱掉所有的支配，不管是老师、家庭还是社会的支配，由此作为个体，他就可以在爱和良善中绽放。在这种帮助学生走向自由的过程中，教育者也在改变他自己的价值观；他同样也会开始摆脱"我"和"我的"，他也会在爱和良善中绽放。这种相互教育的过程，就会创造出一种完全不同的师生关系。

The child is influenced by the people and the things about him, and the right kind of educator should help him to uncover these influences and their true worth. Right values are not discovered through the authority of society or tradition; only individual thoughtfulness can reveal them.

If one understands this deeply, one will encourage the student from the very beginning to awaken insight into present-day individual and social values. One will encourage him to seek out, not any particular set of values, but the true value of all things. One will help him to be fearless, which is to be free of all domination, whether by the teacher, the family or society, so that as an individual he can flower in love and goodness. In thus helping the student towards freedom, the educator is changing his own values also; he too is beginning to be rid of the "me" and the "mine", he too is flowering in love and goodness. This process of mutual education creates an altogether different relationship between the teacher and the student.

任何支配或强迫都会直接阻碍自由和智慧。正确的教育者在社会上没有权威，也没有权力；他超越了社会的法令与约束。如果我们要帮助学生，让他摆脱自己的障碍——这些障碍是他自己和他的环境制造出来的——我们就必须了解每一种强迫和支配的形式，然后抛弃它们；但如果教育者自己也未能摆脱所有有害的权威，那么上述事情就无法实现了。

追随他人，不管那个人多么伟大，都阻碍了对于自我的运作方式的发现；追求某个现成乌托邦的承诺，使心灵完全觉察不到其自身渴望安慰、渴望权威、渴望他人帮助的封闭性活动。牧师、政客、律师、军人都在那儿"帮助"我们；但这种帮助破坏了智慧和自由。我们需要的并不是来自外界的帮助，我们不需要去乞求帮助。当我们谦虚地献身于工作，当我们坦诚开放地去了解我们日常生活的苦恼和突发事件时，帮助就会不求自来了。

Domination or compulsion of any kind is a direct hindrance to freedom and intelligence. The right kind of educator has no authority, no power in society; he is beyond the edicts and sanctions of society. If we are to help the student to be free from his hindrances, which have been created by himself and by his environment, then every form of compulsion and domination must be understood and put aside; and this cannot be done if the educator is not also freeing himself from all crippling authority.

To follow another, however great, prevents the discovery of the ways of the self; to run after the promise of some ready-made Utopia makes the mind utterly unaware of the enclosing action of its own desire for comfort, for authority, for someone else's help. The priest, the politician, the lawyer, the soldier, are all there to "help" us; but such help destroys intelligence and freedom. The help we need does not lie outside ourselves. We do not have to beg for help; it comes without our seeking it when we are humble in our dedicated work, when we are open to the understanding of our daily trials and accidents.

我们必须避免有意识或无意识地去渴望支持与鼓励，因为这种渴望会制造出它自身的反应——这种反应常常是令人满足的。有人鼓励我们、引导我们、安抚我们，这是非常令人舒服的事；然而这种求助于他人，把他人当成向导和权威的习惯，很快就会变成我们体系中的一剂毒药。当我们依赖于他人的引导时，我们就会忘记自己的初衷——那就是唤醒个体的自由和智慧。

所有的权威都是一种障碍，因此最重要的就是，教育者不应该成为学生的权威。权威的建立既是一个有意识的过程，也是一个无意识的过程。

学生对一切都感到不确定，他还在摸索中，但老师对自己的知识确信无疑，经验也很丰富。老师的强势和肯定带给了学生一种保证，学生会倾向于沐浴在那种阳光之下；但这种保证既不持久也不真实。一个有意或无意地鼓励依赖的老师，永远不会对学生有多大帮助。他也许可以用自己的知识来压倒他们，用他的人格魅力来迷倒学生，但他并不是正确的教育者，因为他的知识和经验已经成了他的沉迷之物、他的安全感和他的牢笼；除非他自己摆脱了它们，否则他无法帮助学生成为完整的人。

We must avoid the conscious or unconscious craving for support and encouragement, for such craving creates its own response, which is always gratifying. It is comforting to have someone to encourage us, to give us a lead, to pacify us; but this habit of turning to another as a guide, as an authority, soon becomes a poison in our system. The moment we depend on another for guidance, we forget our original intention, which was to awaken individual freedom and intelligence.

All authority is a hindrance, and it is essential that the educator should not become an authority for the student. The building up of authority is both a conscious and an unconscious process.

The student is uncertain, groping, but the teacher is sure in his knowledge, strong in his experience. The strength and certainty teacher give assurance to the student, who tends to bask in that but such assurance is neither lasting nor true. A teacher who or unconsciously encourages dependence can never be of great students. He may overwhelm them with his knowledge, dazzle them with his personality, but he is not the right kind of educator because his knowledge and experiences are his addiction, his security, his prison; and until he himself is free of them, he cannot help his students to be integrated human beings.

要成为正确的教育者，老师必须不断地把自己从书本和实验室中解脱出来；他必须永远保持警惕，确保学生不要把他当成榜样、理想或权威。当老师渴望在他的学生身上实现自己，当学生的成功就是他的成功时，那么他的教学就是一种延续自我的形式，这对于自我了解和自由是有害的。正确的教育者必须觉察到所有这些障碍，从而帮助他的学生不仅仅摆脱他的权威，也摆脱掉他们自己各种自我封闭的追求。

不幸的是，当遇到需要去了解一个问题的时候，大多数老师并没有把学生当成一个平等的伙伴，他们凭借高高在上的地位去指导学生——学生是远远在他们之下的。这种关系只会加强老师和学生双方各自的恐惧。是什么制造了这种不平等的关系？是不是因为老师害怕被摸清底细？他与学生保持着一段有尊严的距离，是不是为了护卫他的脆弱与重要性？这种高高在上的冷漠和高傲，绝不可能帮助学生打破那些造成了人与人之间分离的障碍。毕竟，教育者和他的学生是在彼此帮助，从而教育他们自己。

To be the right kind of educator, a teacher must constantly be freeing himself from books and laboratories; he must ever be watchful to see that the students do not make of him an example, an ideal, an authority. When the teacher desires to fulfil himself in his students, when their success is his, then his teaching is a form of self-continuation, which is detrimental to self- knowledge and freedom. The right kind of educator must be aware of all these hindrances in order to help his students to be free, not only from his authority, but from their own self-enclosing pursuits.

Unfortunately, when it comes to understanding a problem, most teachers do not treat the student as an equal partner; from their superior position, they give instructions to the pupil, who is far below them. Such a relationship only strengthens fear in both the teacher and the student. What creates this unequal relationship? Is it that the teacher is afraid of being found out? Does he keep a dignified distance to guard his susceptibilities, his importance? Such superior aloofness in no way helps to break down the barriers that separate individuals. After all, the educator and his pupil are helping each other to educate themselves.

所有的关系都应该成为一种相互间的教育。因为知识、成就和野心所提供的防卫性的孤立只会滋生妒忌和对立,因此正确的教育者必须越过这些他在自己周围所设立的围墙。

正确的教育者只是致力于实现个体的自由和完整,所以他具有深刻的、真正的宗教性。他不属于任何教派、任何组织化的宗教,他摆脱了信仰和仪式,因为他知道它们只是那些制造它们的人经由自身的欲望而投射出来的错觉、想象和迷信。他知道只有当有了自我了解,从而拥有了自由时,真实或上帝才会显现。

那些没有学位的人往往会成为最好的老师,因为他们愿意去尝试;他们并非专家,但他们有兴趣去学习,有兴趣去了解生活。对真正的老师来说,教学并不是一种技巧,而是他的生活方式;就像一个伟大的艺术家,他宁愿挨饿也不会放弃他的创作。除非一个人内心燃烧着这种教学热情,否则他不应该去当老师。最重要的是,他要亲自去发现他有没有这种天赋,而不仅仅是随波逐流地进入教师这一行——只是因为可以靠它来混口饭吃。

All relationship should be a mutual education; and as the isolation afforded by knowledge, by achievement, by ambition, only breeds envy and antagonism, the right kind of educator must transcend these walls with which he surrounds himself.

Because he is devoted solely to the freedom and integration of the individual, the right kind of educator is deeply and truly religious. He does not belong to any sect, to any organized religion; he is free of beliefs and rituals, for he knows that they are only illusions, fancies, superstitions projected by the desires of those who create them. He knows that reality or God comes into being only when there is self-knowledge and therefore freedom.

People who have no academic degrees often make the best because they are willing to experiment; not being specialists, interested in learning, in understanding life. For the true teacher, teaching is not a technique, it is his way of life; like a great artist, he would rather starve than give up his creative work. Unless one has this burning desire to teach, one should not be a teacher. It is of the utmost importance that one discover for oneself whether one has this gift, and not merely drift into teaching because it is a means of livelihood.

只要教书仍旧只是一种职业、一种谋生手段，而不是我们为之奉献的天职，那么在我们自己和这个世界之间就必然会存在一道巨大的鸿沟：我们的家庭生活和我们的工作依然会是分离的、有区别的。只要教育仍旧只是一份平凡无奇的工作，那么个体与个体之间、社会不同阶层之间就不可避免地会有冲突和敌意；我们将会有越来越多的竞争、对个人野心的无情追求，以及不断建立起国家和种族的区分——这种区分制造了对立和无尽的战争。

然而，如果我们致力于让自己成为正确的教育者，我们就不会制造出家庭生活和学校生活之间的阻隔，因为无论在什么地方，我们关心的都是自由和智慧。我们会对穷人的孩子和富人的孩子一视同仁，把每个孩子都看作是一个有着自己独特个性、遗传和抱负等的个体。我们关心的不是某个阶层的人，不是权势阶层或弱势群体，我们关心的是个体的自由和完整。

As long as teaching is only a profession, a means of livelihood, a dedicated vocation, there is bound to be a wide gap between and ourselves: our home life and our work remain separate and distinct. As long as education is only a job like any other, conflict and enmity among individuals and among the various class levels of society are inevitable; there will be increasing competition, the ruthless pursuit of personal ambition, and the building up of the national and racial divisions which create antagonism and endless wars.

But if we have dedicated ourselves to be the right kind of educators, we do not create barriers between our home life and the life at school, for we are everywhere concerned with freedom and intelligence. We consider equally the children of the rich and of the poor, regarding each child as an individual with his particular temperament, heredity, ambitions, and so on. We are concerned, not with a class, not with the powerful or the weak, but with the freedom and integration of the individual.

献身于正确的教育必须是完全自愿的。它不应该是任何他人劝说或希望获得个人利益的结果；它必须没有那种由于渴望成功与成就而产生的恐惧。让自己认同于学校的成功或失败，仍旧属于个人动机的范畴。如果教书是我们的天职，如果我们把正确的教育视为个体生死攸关的需要，我们就不会允许自己受到阻碍，或者以任何方式被自己或他人的野心转移方向；我们将会为这项工作腾出时间，找出机会，然后着手开始去做它，而不求任何回报、荣誉或名声。那时所有其他的东西——无论是家庭、个人安全感，还是舒适安逸——就变得不那么重要了。

如果我们很真诚地想要做一名正确的老师，我们将会彻底感到不满，因为我们看到没有任何教育方法可以使个体获得自由。某个方法或体系也许可以制约个体，让他接受一套不同的价值观，但无法使他获得自由。

Dedication to the right kind of education must be wholly should not be the result of any kind of persuasion, or of any hope of personal gain; and it must be devoid of the fears that arise from the craving for success and achievement. The identification of oneself with the success or failure of a school is still within the field of personal motive. If to teach is one's vocation, if one looks upon the right kind of education as a vital need for the individual, then one will not allow oneself to be hindered or in any way sidetracked either by one's own ambitions or by those of another; one will find time and opportunity for this work, and will set about it without seeking reward, honour or fame. Then all other things — family, personal security, comfort — become of secondary importance.

If we are in earnest about being the right kind of teachers, we shall be thoroughly dissatisfied, because we see that no educational method can free the individual. A method or a system may condition him to a different set of values, but it cannot make him free.

我们也必须非常小心，不要陷入自己特有的体系中——心智在不停地建造这种我们个人的体系。拥有一套行为、行动的模式是非常方便和安全的做法，这就是心智会躲避到它公式化的行动中去的原因。持续保持警觉是一件麻烦吃力的事，而制订一种方法然后遵循它却不需要动什么脑筋。

习惯与重复助长了心灵的怠惰，我们需要一种冲击来唤醒心灵——我们把这种冲击称为"问题"。我们试图根据自己老一套的解释、辩护和谴责来解决这个难题，而所有这些都会让心灵再度沉睡。心灵不断陷入这种怠惰中，而正确的教育者，不但会终止自己内心的怠惰，同样也会帮助他的学生去觉察怠惰。

有人或许会问："我要如何才能成为正确的教育者？"毫无疑问，询问"如何"表明了心灵的不自由，表明了心灵是胆怯的，它在寻求某种利益和结果。希望成为某个大人物，以及由此而来的努力，只会让心灵去遵从那个它所渴望的目标，然而一颗自由的心灵则是在不断地观察、学习，从而打破它自己所投射的种种障碍。

One has to be very watchful also not to fall into one's own system, which the mind is ever building. To have a pattern of conduct, of action, is a convenient and safe procedure, and that is why the mind takes shelter within its formulations. To be constantly alert is bothersome and exacting, but to develop and follow a method does not demand thought.

Repetition and habit encourage the mind to be sluggish; a shock is needed to awaken it, which we then call a problem. We try to solve this problem according to our well-worn explanations, justifications and condemnations, all of which puts the mind back to sleep again. In this form of sluggishness the mind is constantly being caught, and the right kind of educator not only puts an end to it within himself, but also helps his students to be aware of it.

Some may ask, "How does one become the right kind of educator? " Surely, to ask "how" indicates, not a free mind, but a mind that is timorous, that is seeking an advantage, a result. The hope and the effort to something only makes the mind conform to the desired end, while a free mind is constantly watching, learning, and therefore breaking through its self-projected hindrances.

自由就在起点，它并不是一个最后才获得的东西。当一个人问"如何"的时候，他就会面临各种难以逾越的困难，然而渴望献身于教育的老师永远不会问这个问题，因为他知道没有任何方法能让我们变成正确的教育者。如果我们怀有极大的兴趣，我们就不会去寻求一种能够确保我们达到预期结果的方法。

有任何体系可以让我们变得智慧吗？我们也许经过了某个体系的培训，取得了学位，等等；但这样我们就能成为教育者了吗，还是说我们仅仅只是那个体系的化身？寻求奖赏，想要被称为杰出的教育者，就是在渴望认可和赞美。虽然获得欣赏和鼓励常常是令人愉快的，然而，如果我们要靠它来维持我们的兴趣，它就会变成麻醉药，很快令我们感到厌倦。期望欣赏和鼓励是很不成熟的表现。

要创造出任何新事物，就必须要有警觉和能量，而不是争吵和争论。如果某人在自己的工作中感到沮丧、失望，那么随之而来的常常就是厌烦和疲惫。如果一个人没有兴趣，他显然就不应该再继续教书了。

Freedom is at the beginning, it is not something to be gained at the end. The moment one asks "how", one is confronted with insurmountable difficulties, and the teacher who is eager to dedicate his life to education will never ask this question, for he knows that there is no method by which one can become the right kind of educator. If one is vitally interested, one does not ask for a method that will assure one of the desired result.

Can any system make us intelligent? We may go through the kind of a system, acquire degrees, and so on; but will we then be educators, or merely the personifications of a system? To seek reward, to want to be called an outstanding educator, is to crave recognition and praise; and while it is sometimes agreeable to be appreciated and encouraged, if one depends upon it for one's sustained interest, it becomes a drug of which one soon wearies. To expect appreciation and encouragement is quite immature.

If anything new is to be created, there must be alertness and energy, not bickerings and wrangles. If one feels frustrated in one's work, then boredom and weariness generally follow. If one is not interested, one should obviously not go on teaching.

但为什么我们的老师常常会缺乏强烈的兴趣？是什么导致了他们的沮丧、失望？之所以会沮丧、失望，不是因为我们被环境强迫着去做这做那，而是因为我们不知道自己真正想要做的事。因为困惑，所以我们任由他人摆布，最后就陷入一些对我们完全没有吸引力的事情中。

如果教书是我们真正的天职，我们也许会暂时感到挫败，因为我们尚未看到可以摆脱如今教育的混乱状况的途径；然而一旦当我们看到并理解了正确教育的含义，我们就会再次获得所有必要的动力和热情。这无关意志或决心，而在于感知和了解。

如果教书成为一个人的天职，如果他认识到正确教育的巨大重要性，他就必定会做一名正确的教育者，却不需要遵循任何方法。如果我们要实现个体的自由与完整，正确的教育是必不可少的——理解这一点就会带来我们自身的彻底转变。如果我们意识到，只有通过正确的教育才会有人类的和平与幸福，我们很自然地就会把自己的一生和兴趣都奉献给它了。

But why is there so often a lack of vital interest among causes one to feel frustrated? Frustration is not the result of being forced by circumstances to do this or that; it arises when we do not know for ourselves what it is that we really want to do. Being confused, we get pushed around, and finally land in something which has no appeal for us at all.

If teaching is our true vocation, we may feel temporarily because we have not seen a way out of this present educational confusion; but the moment we see and understand the implications of the right kind of education, we shall have again all the necessary drive and enthusiasm. It is not a matter of will or resolution, but of perception and understanding.

If teaching is one's vocation, and if one perceives the grave importance of the right kind of education, one cannot help but be the right kind of educator. There is no need to follow any method. The very fact of understanding that the right kind of education is indispensable if we are to achieve the freedom and integration of the individual, brings about a fundamental change in oneself. If one becomes aware that there can be peace and happiness for man only through right education, then one will naturally give one's whole life and interest to it.

一个人去教书是因为他想要孩子的内在变得富有,内在的富有将会使他对外在的财富有一个正确的价值观。没有内在的富有,世俗的事物就会变得过分重要,从而导致各种形式的毁灭与痛苦。教书是为了鼓励学生找到他真正的天职,并且避开那些助长人与人之间对立的职业。教书是为了帮助年轻人走向自知,没有自知就不会有和平与持久的幸福。教书并不是自我实现,而是自我舍弃。

没有正确的教育,错觉就会被误认为真实,于是个体的内心就会一直处于冲突状态,因此在他和别人的关系中——这种关系就是社会——也会有冲突。一个人去当老师是因为他看到唯有自我了解才能带来一颗平静的心灵,而不是宗教组织的教条和仪式。而只有当超越了"我"和"我的",创造、真理和上帝才会显现。

One teaches because one wants the child to be rich inwardly, which will result in his giving right value to possessions. Without inner richness, worldly things become extravagantly important, leading to various forms of destruction and misery. One teaches to encourage the student to find his true vocation, and to avoid those occupations that foster antagonism between man and man. One teaches to help the young towards self-knowledge, without which there can be no peace, no lasting happiness. One's teaching is not self-fulfilment, but self-abnegation.

Without the right kind of teaching, illusion is taken for reality, and then the individual is ever in conflict within himself, and therefore there is conflict in his relationship with others, which is society. One teaches because one sees that self-knowledge alone, and not the dogmas and rituals of organized religion, can bring about a tranquil mind; and that creation, truth, God, comes into being only when the "me" and the "mine" are transcended.

第七章
性与婚姻

CHAPTER VII
SEX AND MARRIAGE

如同其他人类问题一样，我们的情欲和性冲动也是一个非常复杂和困难的问题，而如果教育者自己还没有深入探究过它，并且看清它的诸多含义，他又怎么去帮助他教育的对象呢？如果父母或老师自己都在性问题上纠缠不清，他又如何去引导孩子呢？如果我们自己都不了解这整个问题的意义，我们还能帮助孩子吗？教育者以何种方式将他对性的理解传授给学生，取决于教育者自己内心的状态，取决于他已经渐渐冷静下来了，还是正欲火中烧。

那么，为什么对我们大多数人来说，性会成为一个充满困惑和冲突的问题呢？为什么它会变成我们生活中的主导因素？其中的一个主要原因，就是我们没有创造性；而我们之所以没有创造性，是因为我们整个社会和道德的文化，也包括我们的教育方法都是建立在智性的发展之上的。性问题的解决，在于了悟到智性的活动是无法产生创造的。相反，只有当智性安静下来时，才会有创造。

Like other human problems, the problem of our passions and sexual urges is a complex and difficult one, and if the educator himself has not deeply probed into it and seen its many implications, how can he help those he is educating? If the parent or the teacher is himself caught up in the turmoils of sex, how can he guide the child? Can we help the children if we ourselves do not understand the significance of this whole problem? The manner in which the educator imparts an understanding of sex depends on the state of his own mind; it depends on whether he is gently dispassionate, or consumed by his own desires.

Now, why is sex to most of us a problem, full of confusion and conflict? Why has it become a dominant factor in our lives? One of the main reasons is that we are not creative; and we are not creative because our whole social and moral culture, as well as our educational methods, are based on development of the intellect. The solution to this problem of sex lies in understanding that creation does not occur through the functioning of the intellect. On the contrary, there is creation only when the intellect is still.

智性或头脑本身只会重复、回忆，它在不断地编织着新词语，重新排列旧词语；因为我们大多数人都只是通过头脑来感受和体验，所以我们只是活在词语中，活在机械性的重复中。很显然这并非创造；由于我们没有创造性，所以留给我们唯一的创造手段就是性。性是属于头脑的，而属于头脑的事物必定要让自己得到满足，否则它就会感到挫败。

我们的思想和生活是聪明的、贫瘠的、虚伪的、空虚的；在感情上，我们感到饥渴；在宗教和智力上，我们是重复的、迟钝的；在社会、政治和经济上，我们则被严加管理和控制。我们并不幸福，我们没有活力，也没有喜悦；无论是在家里、在生意场上、在教堂里，还是在学校里，我们从未体验过一种创造性的存在状态，我们的日常思想和行动中缺乏一种深层次的释放。由于在各个方面都受到围困和约束，于是性很自然地就成了我们唯一的发泄口，我们一次次地寻求性体验，是因为它可以暂时提供那种极乐状态，那种当"自我"不存在时所出现的状态。构成问题的并不是性，而是那份想要再次体验极乐状态、想要获取和维持性快感或其他快感的渴望。

The intellect, the mind as such, can only repeat, recollect, it is constantly spinning new words and rearranging old ones; and as most of us feel and experience only through the brain, we live exclusively on words and mechanical repetitions. This is obviously not creation; and since we are uncreative, the only means of creativeness left to us is sex. Sex is of the mind, and that which is of the mind must fulfil itself or there is frustration.

Our thoughts, our lives are bright, arid, hollow, empty; are starved, religiously and intellectually we are repetitive, dull; politically and economically we are regimented, controlled. We happy people, we are not vital, joyous; at home, in business, at church, at school, we never experience a creative state of being, there is no deep release in our daily thought and action. Caught and held from all sides, naturally sex becomes our only outlet, an experience to be sought again and again because it momentarily offers that state of happiness which comes when there is absence of self. It is not sex that constitutes a problem, but the desire to recapture the state of happiness, to gain and maintain pleasure, whether sexual or any other.

我们真正在寻找的，其实是这种忘却自我的强烈激情，这种与某个事物的认同，在其中我们可以彻底失去自我。因为自我是渺小的、卑微的，它是痛苦的根源，于是有意识或无意识地，我们想要在个体或集体的兴奋狂欢中，在崇高的思想中，或者在粗俗的感官刺激中失去自我。

当我们寻求逃避自己时，逃避的手段就会变得非常重要，然后这些手段也成了令我们痛苦的问题。除非我们探究并了解这些阻止了创造性生活的障碍——创造性的生活就是从自我中解脱——否则我们将无法了解性的问题。

阻止了创造性的生活的障碍之一便是恐惧，保持体面就是那种恐惧的表现。那些体面人，那些受世俗道德束缚的人，他们并没有觉察到生活丰富和深刻的意义。他们被封闭在他们自身"正直"的围墙里，而无法看到更远的地方。他们所戴的那种道德的有色眼镜是基于理想和宗教信仰的，和真实现状毫无关系；当他们躲在它后面寻求庇护，他们就是活在自己幻想的世界里。尽管他们有着自愿接受的、令人满意的道德，但这些体面人同样也处于困惑、痛苦和冲突之中。

What we are really searching for is this intense passion of self-forgetfulness, this identification with something in which we can lose ourselves completely. Because the self is small, petty and a source of pain, consciously or unconsciously we want to lose ourselves in individual or collective excitement, in lofty thoughts, or in some gross form of sensation.

When we seek to escape from the self, the means of escape important, and then they also become painful problems to us. investigate and understand the hindrances that prevent creative living, which is freedom from self, we shall not understand the problem of sex.

One of the hindrances to creative living is fear, and respectability is a manifestation of that fear. The respectable, the morally bound, are not aware of the full and deep significance of life. They are enclosed between the walls of their own righteousness and cannot see beyond them. Their stained-glass morality, based on ideals and religious beliefs, has nothing to do with reality; and when they take shelter behind it, they are living in the world of their own illusions. In spite of their self-imposed and gratifying morality, the respectable also are in confusion, misery and conflict.

恐惧是我们渴望安全的产物，它使我们去遵从、模仿、服从于支配，因此它阻碍了创造性的生活。创造性的生活就是活在自由中，活在自由中就是不再有任何恐惧；而只有当心灵没有陷入欲望以及欲望的满足中时，才会有一种创造性的状态。只有通过细致入微地观察自己的心灵和思想，我们才能揭开自己欲望的种种隐秘的方式。我们越是深思熟虑、越是充满爱，支配我们心灵的欲望就越少。只有当我们没有爱时，感官刺激才会变成一个使人精疲力竭的问题。

要理解感官刺激的问题，我们不应该只从任何一个单一的角度去处理它，而是应该从方方面面去看待它——从教育、宗教、社会和道德各个角度去看。对我们来说，感官刺激几乎已经变成了唯一重要的事，因为我们是如此过度地强调感官价值。

通过书籍、广告、电影和无数其他的形式，我们在不断地强调着各种感官刺激。政治游行、宗教盛会、剧院和其他各种形式的娱乐消遣，这一切都在鼓励我们去寻找生活中不同层面上的感官刺激；而我们则在这种鼓励中感到无比快乐。人类千方百计地开发肉欲，同时却崇尚贞洁的理想。于是我们内心就产生了一种矛盾，而说来也奇怪，这种矛盾本身也会令人感到刺激。

Fear, which is the result of our desire to be secure, makes us imitate and submit to domination, and therefore it prevents creative living. To live creatively is to live in freedom, which is to be without fear; and there can be a state of creativeness only when the mind is not caught up in desire and the gratification of desire. It is only by watching our own hearts and minds with delicate attention that we can unravel the hidden ways of our desire. The more thoughtful and affectionate we are, the less desire dominates the mind. It is only when there is no love that sensation becomes a consuming problem.

To understand this problem of sensation, we shall have to it, not from any one direction, but from every side, the religious, the social and the moral. Sensations have become almost exclusively important to us because we lay such overwhelming emphasis on sensate values.

Through books, through advertisements, through the cinema, and in many other ways, various aspects of sensation are constantly being stressed. The political and religious pageants, the theatre and other forms of amusement, all encourage us to seek stimulation at different levels of our being; and we delight in this encouragement. Sensuality is being developed in every possible way, and at the same time, the ideal of chastity is upheld. A contradiction is thus built up within us; and strangely enough, this very contradiction is stimulating.

只有当我们了解到这种对感官刺激的追求——这种追求是心灵的主要活动之一——快感、刺激和暴力才不会成为我们生活中的显著特征。因为我们没有爱，所以性和对感官刺激的追求才会变成令人精疲力竭的问题。当有了爱，就有了贞洁；然而，那个努力去变得贞洁的人并不是贞洁的。美德伴随着自由而来，当我们了解了真实现状时，美德就会出现。

年轻的时候，我们都有着强烈的性冲动，但大多数人都试图通过控制和约束它们来处理这些欲望，因为我们觉得如果没有某种约束，我们就会变得非常淫荡、好色。组织化的宗教非常注重我们的性道德；然而他们允许我们沉溺在妒忌和狡猾的残忍中，允许我们去追求权力与成功。为什么他们如此关心这种特定类型的道德，却不去抨击一下剥削、贪婪和战争呢？难道不是因为宗教组织——我们所创造的环境的一部分——本身就是依靠我们的恐惧、希望、妒忌和分裂而得以存在的吗？所以在宗教领域里，就像在所有其他领域一样，心灵也被困在它自身欲望的种种投射里。

It is only when we understand the pursuit of sensation, which is one of the major activities of the mind, that pleasure, excitement and violence cease to be a dominant feature in our lives. It is because we do not love, that sex, the pursuit of sensation, has become a consuming problem. When there is love, there is chastity; but he who tries to be chaste, is not. Virtue comes with freedom, it comes when there is an understanding of what is.

When we are young, we have strong sexual urges, and most of us try to deal with these desires by controlling and disciplining them, because we think that without some kind of restraint we shall become lustful. Organized religions are much concerned about our sexual morality; but they allow us to indulge in envy and crafty ruthlessness, and to pursue power and success. Why should they be so concerned with this particular type of morality, and not attack exploitation, greed and war? Is it not because organized religions, being part of the environment which we have created, depend for their very existence on our fears and hopes, on our envy and separatism? So, in the religious field as in every other, the mind is held in the projections of its own desires.

只要我们不能深入理解欲望的整个过程，现有的婚姻制度，不管是东方的还是西方的，就无法提供关于性问题的解答。爱不是通过签订一纸婚约而引发的，它也不是建立在交换彼此的满足、安全感和安慰之上的。所有这些东西都属于头脑，而这就是爱在我们的生活中只占据了极小部分的原因。爱并不属于头脑，它完全独立于思想，以及思想那狡猾的算计和自我防卫的需求及反应。当有了爱，性永远不会成为问题——正是因为缺乏爱才导致了性的问题。

构成问题的，是头脑的种种障碍和逃避，而不是性或其他什么东西；所以重要的是要了解头脑的运作过程，了解那些吸引它的东西和它所排斥的东西，以及它对于美和丑的反应。我们应该观察自己，觉察到我们是如何看待他人的，我们是怎样去看一个男人或女人的。我们应当看到，当家庭被当作一种自我永存的手段，当家庭是为了彰显自我的重要性时，它就会成为制造分离和反社会活动的中心。家庭和财富，当它们是以自我及其日益狭隘的欲望和追求为中心时，就会沦为权力和支配的工具，成为个体与社会之间冲突的源头。

As long as there is no deep understanding of the whole process of desire, the institution of marriage as it now exists, whether in the East or in the West, cannot provide the answer to the sexual problem. Love is not induced by the signing of a contract, nor is it based on an exchange of gratification, nor on mutual security and comfort. All these things are of the mind, and that is why love occupies so small a place in our lives. Love is not of the mind, it is wholly independent of thought with its cunning calculations, its self-protective demands and reactions. When there is love, sex is never a problem — it is the lack of love that creates the problem.

The hindrances and escapes of the mind constitute the problem, and not sex or any other specific issue; and that is why it is important to understand the mind's process, its attractions and repulsions, its responses to beauty, to ugliness. We should observe ourselves, become aware of how we regard people, how we look at men and women. We should see that the family becomes a centre of separatism and of anti-social activities when it is used as a means of self-perpetuation, for the sake of one's self-importance. Family and property, when centred on the self with its ever-narrowing desires and pursuits, become the instruments of power and domination, a source of conflict between the individual and society.

所有这些人类问题的困难就在于，我们自己作为父母和老师，已经变得如此彻底的疲倦和绝望，内心完全混乱，失去了平静；生活沉重地压在我们身上，我们想要求得安慰，我们渴望被人所爱。在内心贫乏、不充实的情况下，我们又如何希望能带给孩子正确的教育呢？

这就是为什么主要的问题并不在于学生，而在于教育者；如果我们想要有能力去教育别人，我们必须先净化自己的心灵和头脑。如果教育者自己都是混乱的、扭曲的、迷失在自身欲望的迷宫里，他又怎么能传授智慧，或者帮助他人走上正途呢？我们并不是机器——可以让专家们来研究了解然后修好；我们是一长串各种影响和突发事件的产物，每个人都必须亲自去揭示和了解自己本性中的混乱。

The difficulty in all these human questions is that we ourselves, the parents and teachers, have become so utterly weary and hopeless, altogether confused and without peace; life weighs heavily upon us, and we be comforted, we want to be loved. Being poor and insufficient within ourselves, how can we hope to give the right kind of education to the child?

That is why the major problem is not the pupil, but the educator; our own hearts and minds must be cleansed if we are to be capable of educating others. If the educator himself is confused, crooked, lost in a maze of his own desires, how can he impart wisdom or help to make straight the way of another? But we are not machines to be understood and repaired by experts; we are the result of a long series of influences and accidents, and each one has to unravel and understand for himself the confusion of his own nature.

第八章
艺术、美和创造

CHAPTER VIII

ART , BEAUTY AND CREATION

我们大部分人都在不断地试图逃避自己,由于艺术提供了一种可敬与简便的逃避途径,于是,它在很多人的生活中扮演着一个重要的角色。因为渴望忘却自我,一些人转向了艺术,另一些人选择了酗酒,同时还有一些人选择了追随那些神秘和虚幻的宗教教义。

当我们有意识或无意识地利用某个东西来逃避自己时,我们就会对它上瘾。依赖一个人、一首诗,或者无论什么东西,把它作为解除我们担忧和焦虑的一种手段,虽然可以暂时令人感到充实,却只会在我们的生活中制造出更深的冲突和矛盾。

有冲突的地方,创造性的状态便无法存在。因此,正确的教育应当帮助个体去面对他自己的种种问题,而不是美化那些逃避方式,它应该帮助他去了解和消除冲突,因为只有那样,创造性的状态才会出现。

脱离了生活的艺术并没有太大意义。当艺术与我们的日常生活是分离的,当我们本能的生活和我们在画布、大理石或文字上的努力工作之间存在一道鸿沟时,艺术就仅仅成了我们想要逃避自己真实模样的肤浅欲望的表达。要在这道鸿沟上架起桥梁是很难的,特别是对那些天赋异禀、精于技巧的人而言。然而,只有在这道鸿沟上架起桥梁,我们的生活才会变得完整,艺术才会成为我们自身完整的表达。

Most of us are constantly trying to escape from ourselves; and as a respectable and easy means of doing so, it plays a significant part in the lives of many people. In the desire for self-forgetfulness, some turn to art, others take to drink, while still others follow mysterious and fanciful religious doctrines.

When, consciously or unconsciously, we use something to ourselves, we become addicted to it. To depend on a person, a what you will, as a means of release from our worries and anxieties, though momentarily enriching, only creates further conflict and contradiction in our lives.

The state of creativeness cannot exist where there is conflict, and the right kind of education should therefore help the individual to face his problems and not glorify the ways of escape; it should help him to understand and eliminate conflict, for only then can this state of creativeness come into being.

Art divorced from life has no great significance. When art is separate from our daily living, when there is a gap between our instinctual life and our efforts on canvas, in marble or in words, then art becomes merely an expression of our superficial desire to escape from the reality of what is. To bridge this gap is very arduous, especially for those who are gifted and technically proficient; but it is only when the gap is bridged that our life becomes integrated and art an integral expression of ourselves.

头脑具有制造幻觉的力量，不了解它的运作方式，去寻找灵感就会招致自我欺骗。灵感是在我们保持开放的时候出现的，而不是在我们追求它的时候。试图通过任何形式的刺激去获取灵感，就会导致各种错觉。

除非我们明白存在的意义，否则才能或天赋只会强调自我及其渴望，并且赋予它们重要性。它往往会让个体变得以自我为中心和分离孤立；他会觉得自己是一个与众不同的人，是高人一等的，这一切都滋生了种种弊害，导致了无尽的冲突和痛苦。自我是由一大堆"存在"组成的，每个"存在"都在反对着其他的"存在"。它是一个充满矛盾欲望的战场，一个"我"与"非我"持续斗争的中心。只要我们依然重视自我、重视"我"和"我的"，那么我们的内心和这个世界就会有越来越多的冲突。

一个真正的艺术家超越了自我的虚荣和自我的野心。而拥有杰出的艺术表现力，却陷入世俗的窠臼中，会导致一种矛盾和冲突的生活。当我们把赞美和奉承放在心上时，就会使自我膨胀并且破坏感受力。任何领域中对成功的崇拜，很显然都有损于智慧。

Mind has the power to create illusion; and without understanding its ways, to seek inspiration is to invite self-deception. Inspiration comes when we are open to it, not when we are courting it. To attempt to gain inspiration through any form of stimulation leads to all kinds of delusions.

Unless one is aware of the significance of existence, capacity or gift gives emphasis and importance to the self and its cravings. It tends to make the individual self-centred and separative; he feels himself to be an entity apart, a superior being, all of which breeds many evils and causes ceaseless strife and pain. The self is a bundle of many entities, each opposed to the others. It is a battlefield of conflicting desires, a centre of constant struggle between the "mine" and the "not-mine"; and as long as we give importance to the self, to the "me" and the "mine", there will be increasing conflict within ourselves and in the world.

A true artist is beyond the vanity of the self and its ambitions. To have the power of brilliant expression, and yet be caught in worldly ways, makes for a life of contradiction and strife. Praise and adulation, when taken to heart, inflate the ego and destroy receptivity, and the worship of success in any field is obviously detrimental to intelligence.

任何助长了孤立的爱好或才能，任何形式的自我认同——无论它多么令人兴奋——都会扭曲敏感性的表达，从而导致麻木无感。当天赋变成个人的东西，当强调"我"和"我的"——"我"画的，"我"写的，"我"发明的时，敏感性就会被钝化。只有当我们在与他人、与事物、与自然的关系中时时刻刻地觉察到我们自己的思想和感受时，心灵才是开放的、柔韧的，不会受缚于自我防卫的需要和追求；唯有那时才会有一种不被自我阻碍的、对丑陋和美丽事物的敏感。

对美与丑的敏感并不是经由依恋而来的；它是当没有了自我制造的冲突以后，伴随着爱而出现的。当我们内在贫穷时，我们便会沉溺于各种形式的外在展示——炫耀财富、权力和自己拥有的东西；当我们心灵空虚时，我们就会去收集各种物品。如果我们有这个经济条件，我们会在自己周围摆满我们认为美丽的东西，而正因为我们对这些东西过分重视，所以我们要对无数的不幸与毁灭负责。

Any tendency or talent which makes for isolation, any form identification, however stimulating, distorts the expression of sensitivity and brings about insensitivity. Sensitivity is dulled when gift becomes personal, when importance is given to the "me" and the "mine"— I paint, I write, I invent. It is only when we are aware of every movement of our own thought and feeling in our relationship with people, with things and with nature, that the mind is open, pliable, not tethered to self-protective demands and pursuits; and only then is there sensitivity to the ugly and the beautiful, unhindered by the self.

Sensitivity to beauty and to ugliness does not come about attachment; it comes with love, when there are no self-created When we are inwardly poor, we indulge in every form of outward show, in wealth, power and possessions. When our hearts are empty, we collect things. If we can afford it, we surround ourselves with objects that we consider beautiful, and because we attach enormous importance to them, we are responsible for much misery and destruction.

贪婪之心并不是对美的热爱，它来自对安全的渴望，而变得安全就是变得麻木无感。对安全的渴望造成了恐惧，它开启了一种孤立化的过程——也就是在我们周围建立起抵抗的围墙，而这些围墙阻止了所有的敏感性。不管那个对象有多么美丽，它很快就失去了对我们的吸引力；我们渐渐习惯于它，那份曾经的喜悦于是变得空虚和无趣。美仍旧在那儿，但我们不再对它保持开放，它已经被我们单调乏味的日常生活吞没了。

因为我们的心灵是干涸的，因为我们已经忘记了如何善以待人，如何去仰望繁星、凝视树木、欣赏水中的倒影，所以我们才需要借助绘画、珠宝、书籍和无穷无尽的娱乐来获得刺激。我们不断地寻求新的刺激、新的兴奋点，我们渴望不断增长的各类感官刺激。正是这种渴望及其满足使得头脑和心灵变得疲倦和迟钝。只要我们还在寻求感官刺激，那些我们称之为美或丑的事物就只会具有非常肤浅的意义。只有当我们能够重新面对一切事物，才会有持久的喜悦，而只要我们还是热衷于自己的各种欲望，这一切就不可能了。渴望感官刺激和满足阻碍了我们去体验那个永远常新的事物。感官刺激可以用钱买到，但对美的热爱是买不到的。

The acquisitive spirit is not the love of beauty; it arises from the desire for security, and to be secure is to be insensitive. The desire to be secure creates fear; it sets going a process of isolation which builds walls of resistance around us, and these walls prevent all sensitivity. However beautiful an object may be, it soon loses its appeal for us; we get used to it, and that which was a joy becomes empty and dull. Beauty is still there, but we are no longer open to it, and it has been absorbed into our monotonous daily existence.

Since our hearts are withered and we have forgotten how to be how to look at the stars, at the trees, at the reflections on the we require the stimulation of pictures and jewels, of books and endless amusements. We are constantly seeking new excitements, new thrills, we crave an ever-increasing variety of sensations. It is this craving and its satisfaction that make the mind and heart weary and dull. As long as we are seeking sensation, the things that we call beautiful and ugly have but a very superficial significance. There is lasting joy only when we are capable of approaching all things afresh — which is not possible as long as we are bound up in our desires. The craving for sensation and gratification prevents the experiencing of that which is always new. Sensations can be bought, but not the love of beauty.

当我们觉察到自己头脑和心灵的空虚,却不逃避到任何一种刺激或感觉中去时;当我们保持完全的开放、高度的敏感时,我们才会有创造,才会发现创造性的喜悦。培养外在的事物却对内在一无所知,这注定会不可避免地建立起那些导致人类毁灭和悲伤的价值观。

学习一项技艺或许可以为我们谋得一份工作,但它无法使我们具有创造性;然而,如果有了喜悦,如果有了创造的火种,我们并不需要去学习表达的技巧,就会找到一种方式来表达自己。当一个人真的想要写一首诗,他就写了,如果他有一些写诗技巧,那当然更好;但如果一个人无话可说,为什么还要去强调诗本身呢——诗只不过是一种交流手段而已。只要心中有爱,我们就不会去寻找遣词造句的方法。

When we are aware of the emptiness of our own minds and hearts without running away from it into any kind of stimulation or sensation, when we are completely open, highly sensitive, only then can there be creation, only then shall we find creative joy. To cultivate the outer without understanding the inner must inevitably build up those values which lead men to destruction and sorrow.

Learning a technique may provide us with a job, but it will not make us creative; whereas, if there is joy, if there is the creative fire, it will find a way to express itself, one need not study a method of expression. When one really wants to write a poem, one writes it, and if one has the technique, so much the better; but why stress what is but a means of communication if one has nothing to say? When there is love in our hearts, we do not search for a way of putting words together.

伟大的艺术家和作家也许是创造者，但我们不是，我们只是观众。我们博览群书，聆听恢宏的乐章，欣赏艺术作品，但是我们从未直接体验过那种崇高的事物；我们的经验永远都是通过一首诗、一幅画或者圣人的人格魅力而来的。想要歌唱，我们心中必须要有一首歌；但因为我们已经失去了那首歌，于是我们便追逐那个歌唱家。没有一个媒介，我们就感到迷失了；然而在我们发现任何事物之前，我们必定要迷失。发现就是创造性的开始；没有了创造性，不管我们做什么，都不会有人类的和平或幸福。

我们认为，如果自己学会了一种方法、技巧或风格的话，我们就能够喜悦地、创造性地生活；然而创造性的喜悦只有当内在富有时才会出现，它永远无法通过任何体系来获得。自我改善是确保"我"与"我的"安全感的另一种方式，它并不是创造性的，也不是对美的热爱。只有当持续不断地觉察到心灵的运作方式，以及它为自己所建造的种种障碍时，创造性才会产生。

创造的自由是伴随着自我了解而来的，但自我了解并不是一种天赋。一个没有什么特殊才华的人也可以具有创造性。创造性是一种存在状态，其中没有自我的冲突与悲伤，心灵也不再陷入欲望的种种需求和追逐之中。

Great artists and great writers may be creators, but we are not, we are mere spectators. We read vast numbers of books, listen to magnificent music, look at works of art, but we never directly experience the sublime; our experience is always through a poem, through a picture, through the personality of a saint. To sing we must have a song in our hearts; but having lost the song, we pursue the singer. Without an intermediary we feel lost; but we must be lost before we can discover anything. Discovery is the beginning of creativeness; and without creativeness, do what we may, there can be no peace or happiness for man.

We think that we shall be able to live happily, creatively, if a method, a technique, a style; but creative happiness comes only when there is inward richness, it can never be attained through any system. Self-improvement, which is another way of assuring the security of the"me"and the"mine", is not creative, nor is it love of beauty. Creativeness comes into being when there is constant awareness of the ways of the mind, and of the hindrances it has built for itself.

The freedom to create comes with self-knowledge; but self-knowledge is not a gift. One can be creative without having any particular talent. Creativeness is a state of being in which the conflicts and sorrows of the self are absent, a state in which the mind is not caught up in the demands and pursuits of desire.

具有创造性并不仅仅是写诗、创作雕像或者生孩子，而是处于那种真理可以显现的状态中。当思想彻底止息时，真理就会显现；而只有当自我不在，当心灵停止造作，也就是当它不再陷入自身的追求中时，思想才会止息。当心灵彻底安静下来时——但不是通过强迫或训练使它静下来；当心灵因为自我停止了活动而变得寂静时，就会有创造。

对美的热爱也可以在一首歌、一个微笑或者在沉默中得以表达，但我们大多数人并不喜欢沉默。我们没有时间去观察小鸟、仰望空中飘过的白云，因为我们太过忙碌于自己的各种追求和欢愉了。如果我们心中没有美，又怎能帮助孩子变得警觉和敏感呢？我们努力对美保持敏感，与此同时却回避丑陋；然而，回避丑陋会导致我们变得不敏感。如果我们想要培养年轻人的敏感性，我们自己必须同保持对美和丑的敏感，我们必须抓住每一个机会，去唤醒他们内心因看见美而产生的喜悦——不仅仅是人类所创造的美，也包括大自然的美。

To be creative is not merely to produce poems, or statues, or children; it is to be in that state in which truth can come into being. Truth comes into being when there is a complete cessation of thought; and thought ceases only when the self is absent, when the mind has ceased to create, that is, when it is no longer caught in its own pursuits. When the mind is utterly still without being forced or trained into quiescence, when it is silent because the self is inactive, then there is creation.

The love of beauty may express itself in a song, in a smile, or in silence; but most of us have no inclination to be silent. We have not the time to observe the birds, the passing clouds, because we are too busy with our pursuits and pleasures. When there is no beauty in our hearts, how can we help the children to be alert and sensitive? We try to be sensitive to beauty while avoiding the ugly; but avoidance of the ugly makes for insensitivity. If we would develop sensitivity in the young, we ourselves must be sensitive to beauty and to ugliness, and must take every opportunity to awaken in them the joy there is in seeing, not only the beauty that man has created, but also the beauty of nature.